Ulrich Giesekus, Bradford M. Smith,
Jürgen Schuster (Eds.)

Global Mental Health and the Church

Interkulturalität & Religion
Intercultural & Religious Studies

Liebenzeller Impulse
zu Mission, Kultur und Religion

herausgegeben von / edited by

Prof. Dr. Jürgen Schuster,
Prof. Dr. Mihamm Kim-Rauchholz
und Prof. Dr. Volker Gäckle

Band / Volume 4

LIT

Global Mental Health and the Church

edited by

Ulrich Giesekus, Bradford M. Smith,
Jürgen Schuster

Cover image: iStockPhoto 451181471 / Urheber: LuckyBusiness

Bibliographic information published by the Deutsche Nationalbibliothek
The Deutsche Nationalbibliothek lists this publication in the Deutsche Nationalbibliografie; detailed bibliographic data are available on the Internet at http://dnb.d-nb.de.

ISBN 978-3-643-90854-4

A catalogue record for this book is available from the British Library

© LIT VERLAG GmbH & Co. KG Wien,
Zweigniederlassung Zürich 2017
Klosbachstr. 107
CH-8032 Zürich
Tel. +41 (0) 44-251 75 05
E-Mail: zuerich@lit-verlag.ch   http://www.lit-verlag.ch
Distribution:
In the UK: Global Book Marketing, e-mail: mo@centralbooks.com
In North America: International Specialized Book Services, e-mail: orders@isbs.com
In Germany: LIT Verlag Fresnostr. 2, D-48159 Münster
Tel. +49 (0) 2 51-620 32 22, Fax +49 (0) 2 51-922 60 99, e-mail: vertrieb@lit-verlag.de
In Austria: Medienlogistik Pichler-ÖBZ, e-mail: mlo@medien-logistik.at
e-books are available at www.litwebshop.de

Table of Contents

Introduction 7
Ulrich Giesekus

Mental Health: The Global Church's Next Great Challenge 11
Bradford M. Smith

Giving Voice to the Voiceless: Collaborative Inquiry in Poor
Communities of Mexico City 31
Saúl Cruz-Valdivieso

Indigenous Christian Counseling in Africa: The Call of the Church to
Care and Counsel as Mission 51
Gladys K. Mwiti

Promoting Mental Health at Congregational Level 63
Beate Jakob

Equipping the Church as a Caring Community 81
Samuel Pfeifer

Global Mental Health Needs and Consequences for Missions 95
Ulrich Giesekus

African Americans and Mental Health: Challenges and Church-Based
Responses 105
Bradford M. Smith and Kathryn A. Cummins

Sickness and Healing in an Animistic Context 115
Simon Herrmann

Contributors 133

Introduction

Ulrich Giesekus

"Global Mental Health and the Role of the Church" was the title of a symposium held at a small Black Forest town Bad Liebenzell in June 2015. Participants from 19 different countries followed the invitation of the "Liebenzell International University", "Liebenzell Mission" and the "Lausanne Committee for Care and Counsel as Mission".

In the three day conference plus a one day post conference meetings, speakers from China, Kenya, Mexico, Switzerland, USA and Germany gathered to present Christian psychology approaches in the Global South. A fascinating variety of international mental health projects was also presented—ranging from trauma care in the civil-war-torn Ukraine to victims of terror in Kenya, initiatives from China to Mississippi and Mexico, from the Saddleback approach to "what every church can do to promote mental health" to working with Ebola survivors in Liberia—and more.

Surprisingly, this was the first scientific conference worldwide to the topic. The term "Global Mental Health" does not immediately ring a bell for most practitioners within the Christian psychotherapy field in the Western world. On the contrary, mental health is often seen as a concern for people who are economically prosperous and live in affluent societies. It is not immediately obvious, why psychology and mental health should be relevant for people who are economically poor, looking for food and shelter, in need of medical care, clean water and basic safety.

It only takes a quick look into the reality of the Global South to realize that this is far from true. For example, confidence and self-esteem are basic conditions for an empowered life—whether one lives on a garbage dump or in an upper-middle-class suburb. Dealing with trauma is vital to raising children in an emotionally stable way. Domestic violence destroys health and working power. Addiction ruins both, emotional and economic development. Sex education helps prevent HIV-infection and genital mutilation. A need for humane conditions for the care of mentally disordered people is not limited to the wealthy. Unfortunately, these crucial concerns have not been addressed properly in the training and practice of developmental helpers, mission workers, or in the development of strategies for helping the poor. "Missions involves a significant amount of mental health work done by people who are not well equipped to deal with psychological disorders."[1] The date of this quote is as revealing as its content: for over 30 years the concern has been voiced but hardly heeded. There seems to be a blind spot to the psychosocial needs of the global poor, as well as to the potential resources that could be generated through proper care. A first major serious effort to put "care and counsel" onto the missions map was made in the 2010 Lausanne Movement meeting in Cape Town (see article by Bradford Smith).

Many of the conference meetings were narrative, there were many intense discussions, and of course scholarly lectures. Some of these can be found in the following chapters. All of the authors are "global players" in the new field of "care and counsel as mission":

Bradford M. Smith has shown excellent leadership both in the global organization of meetings as well as research on the topic of global aspects in psychosocial care. His profound understanding of diverse international contexts of care and interdisciplinary competence make him the right author to be the first contributor. In a second contribution together with Kathryn A. Cummins he also documents the fact that knowledge about intercultural work among poor populations is not limited to the so called Third World but can also be applied within Western cultures.

Saúl Cruz-Valdivieso and his mother, Pilar Cruz are leading the Armonía organization. Only a few weeks after the sudden and tragic death of its founder, Saúl Cruz-Ramos, they presented ways that scientific research can pick up on the idea that the poor are not just passively being studied but can be empowered to actively contribute knowledge toward a better understanding of their situations. This is in line with the general idea of Armonía that empowerment must focus on the resources and potential of poor communities rather than provide help that ultimately may cause dependence and helplessness.

The Kenyian psychologist Gladys Mwiti has developed a trauma care program in Kenya, Oasis Africa, where large numbers of trauma care helpers are trained to different levels. They can react quickly in catastrophic situations and offer help from a qualified first response up to necessary trauma therapy. Gladys Mwiti has profound insights into the integration of Western science, African indigenous tradition and Christian faith.

Beate Jacob is a medical doctor who has shown exceptional leadership in health promotion in many regions of the world. Her conference presenta-

---

[1] Hesselgrave, D. (1986). Culture-sensitive counseling and the Christian mission. *International Bulletin of Missionary Research, 10*, 109–116.

tion of a project among Ebola survivors was encouraging to many, as it became clear that much help and emotional relief is possible even in difficult circumstances. She also documents in an impressive way that rich countries helping poor regions is not a one way road: implementing a community project on depression, largely modeled from African experiences, in a German congregation works well. In fact, we do learn from one another.

Samuel Pfeifer is a key player in the global development of psychiatric care. The Suisse psychiatrist not only holds a medical degree but also degrees in psychology and theology. The former medical director of a psychiatric clinic near Basel is editor of a journal of psychiatry and pastoral care, his books have been translated into ten different languages, and he is now professor of psychiatry and psychotherapy. Among his contributions to the conference was the fundamental summary on "equipping the church as a caring community" which can be found below.

Simon Herrman is presenting an important lesson in intercultural health care. It becomes evident that our culturally different paradigms of understanding health—of course, including mental health—must be understood. Even the most basic terms carry very different meanings and are associated with entirely different reality constructions. He challenges us not only to understand the spiritual underpinnings given to everyday phenomena, but to question our own rationalistic world views and develop a more holistic approach.

My own contribution to the conference, as conference director, was to coordinate the many different contributions and to connect ideas and people. Of course, there were many who contributed behind the scenes and without whom the conference would not have been possible. As it is impossible to present a complete list, I want to select only one other key player: my colleague Jürgen Schuster, head of the Research Center at Liebenzell International University, edited this compendium and was a driving force in the organization and implementation of the entire conference from the first beginnings to the final collection of papers.

At the end of the conference, there was agreement, that this must not be a project which is now finished, but must be part of an ongoing process. Cultural and economic development, the struggle against poverty and misery in this world, must include psychosocial care. Good relationships, positive self-esteem and mental health are basic to improvements of the entire situation in poor and wealthy regions alike.

Some of the conference presenters and hosts (from left to right):
Simon Herrmann, Brad Smith, Judy and Patrick Bailey, Saúl Cruz-Valdivieso,
Henning Freund, Pilar Cruz, Dietmar Roller, Samuel Pfeifer, Gladys Mwiti,
Ulrich Giesekus, Beate Jakob, Thomas Eisinger, Volker Gäckle, Martin Auch.

More than 60 participants from 17 countries
gathered for the consultation.

Mental Health: The Global Church's Next Great Challenge

Bradford M. Smith

I begin this article by asking you to imagine a church anywhere in the world and the community beyond its walls. Now, realize that we know from research in many countries that one in five people in the congregation will be suffering from some kind of mental illness or substance abuse problem. One in five—that's 20% within a year—on average in our churches (National Institute of Mental Health, 2015). Notice that in churches around the world, one in four, *within their lifetime*, will suffer from a mental illness (World Health Organization, 2011).

Of course we know that there is so much more. There are so many other kinds of challenges that people have that fit into this broad category that we call mental health. We struggle with the terminology and may use such terms as personal problems, emotional struggles, psychosocial disorders, and so one. There is so much beyond the common categories of mental illness but they give us an order of magnitude of the challenges people face in life from the cradle to grave. There are problems children face such as autism and attention deficit disorder. Then there is the arena of relational problems: the need for couples and families to receive help and healing in their relationships. There are the psychosocial problems that arise as the result of interpersonal violence or human disasters causing post-traumatic stress disorder. There are so many different kinds of problems including serious illnesses like schizophrenia and bipolar disorder. In the elder years, there are additional challenges for such as types of dementia including Alzheimer's disease.

The Magnitude of the Problem

The magnitude of this issue that I am addressing in this article is huge from a statistical perspective. But it's also huge in terms of the impact it has on people and the level of suffering that it brings. First of all, people with mental health problems die younger (Patel, 2012). In the high income countries, they die up to 25 years earlier. In the lower and middle income countries, it is even more than that (Patel, 2012). There is a tremendous loss of the *quantity* of life.

There is also a loss in the *quality* of life. There is loss in the ability to work, to relate well, to enjoy life. The World Health Organization has tried to quantify this loss in a term they call the DALY (Disability Adjusted Life Years). This is an attempt to quantify the loss in terms of length of life and quality of life that occurs because of mental health disorders. This kind of rough quantification is helpful because it allows us to compare the priority of mental health issues with other public health issues globally.

We find depression alone has become the leading cause of disability worldwide (World Health Organization, 2016). One of the major reasons that people miss work is depression. By the year 2030, it is predicted that depression will be the second highest cause of the disease burden in middle-income countries and the third highest in low-income countries (Patel, 2012). Notice, it is not heart disease, nor diabetes, nor cancer, but depression which is often a hidden contributor to other problems in society.

In these statistics, there is the human impact—the loss—but then there is also the stigma and the shame that accompanies these kinds of problems. People and their families want to hide because of them. We know in some situations that families literally keep their mentally ill relatives locked up and out of sight at home for years at a time.

This leads to another problem. People do not get the treatment that they need. In the higher income countries up to 50% of people do not receive adequate treatment for their mental health problems (Patel, 2012). In the poorer countries it is even worse. Dr. Vikram Patel, the eminent psychiatrist with the World Health Organization suggests that in the poor countries where he works, up to 90% of people with mental health disorders go untreated. So the problem is huge. The question is how can we as followers of Jesus help?

The Biblical Foundation

In the Gospel of Matthew, the Bible says:

> Jesus traveled through all the towns and villages of that area, teaching in the synagogues and announcing the Good News about the Kingdom. And he healed every kind of disease and illness. When he saw the crowds, he had compassion on them because they were confused and helpless, like sheep without a shepherd. (Mt. 9:35-36 NLT)

Jesus proclaimed the good news, the gospel. He healed disease and sickness and he had compassion on the harassed and the helpless. The passage continues that the harvest is plentiful, the workers few, "so pray to the Lord who is in charge of the harvest; ask him to send more workers into his fields" (Mt. 9:38).

When I was a little boy growing up in my country church, we had a mission conference every year and every year the missions committee named this verse about the harvest as the theme verse. In my young mind, I always thought that this harvesting was simply about the harvesting of souls. I thought we were talking strictly about evangelists and evangelism. Then, as I became more and more interested in all of the needs of people and in a more holistic understanding of Scripture I discovered that the harvest includes the healing of people and their diseases, and compassion for them. Certainly, we need workers for this kind of holistic ministry that models the ministry of Jesus himself.

A number of years ago the *Lausanne Theology Working Group* (2007) of the Lausanne Movement (www.lausanne.org) held a symposium on suffering. As part of their summary statement, they wrote: "The claim that Jesus is the truth must be demonstrated in the Christian praxis of attending to human pain and meeting human needs … the praxis of good works" (para. 1.2). As we consider the whole canon of Scripture, both Old Testament and New, we see there is a bridge, a connection between proclaiming the gospel of Jesus as the truth and our practice of compassion and caring.

The Evolution of a New Paradigm

The phrase that we use in the Lausanne Movement for this is "Care and Counsel as Mission." I will unfold the brief history of this term by talking about four cities. The story begins in the town of Reading, Massachusetts in the USA where I lived until recently. In June of 2007, I called a very small "summit conference" of two other people.

One of those people was Dr. Gary Collins, an American psychologist, originally from Canada, who is known as one of the founding fathers of Christian counseling. In addition, there was Dr. Fred Gingrich, a Canadian, who heads the Counseling Division at Denver Seminary in the United States, and directed masters and doctoral programs in Christian counseling in the Philippines for eight years.

We came together to discuss the tremendous needs we were seeing around the world and how we might better stimulate a response and provide training for those needs to be better met. As we began to grapple with this, we realized that, first of all, we had a terminology problem. We struggled with using the term "Christian counseling" for the diverse kinds of responses we were envisioning because we realized that Christian counseling is often pictured in a traditional way as somebody having a nice psychotherapy office and conversing one-on-one for precisely 50 minutes—the classic "fifty minute" psychotherapy hour. We realized that God was addressing mental health needs in rural and urban areas of the world through people offering wonderfully creative, diverse, highly contextualized, culturally-sensitive approaches that went far beyond traditional Christian counseling methods.

We struggled with finding a broader, more inclusive term. When you have Gary Collins at the meeting, a person who has written 140 books, you give them the homework assignment to come up with the right wording. We agreed to think about it overnight and Gary Collins came down to breakfast the next morning and suggested we use the term "care and counsel." I said I had never really heard of that term and Gary said that was exactly why we should use it. We could adapt the term however we wanted to but it would give us a term broader than Christian counseling. So for us, at breakfast that morning, the term "care and counsel" came to describe the many roles that people can play when working globally in counseling-related ministries.

At the Reading meeting, the other terminology problem we observed in the church was that whenever we taught about counseling, missions people always assumed we were talking about counseling missionaries or, what is known as "member care." We would always answer that we knew such work is really important for missionaries and their families around the world who sacrificed much, but that we had a broader vision that we called "care and counsel" and we want to reach out in a missional way to try to help everybody in the world that we can help—not just missionaries, not just church people, but the whole world.

As an example: Last week, I was flying to Johannesburg. A Muslim man sat next to me in the airplane and initially we did not speak. We both sat silently until I pulled out a book that I was reading to prepare for a class I was teaching. The book was a basic book on counseling skills. When I pulled that book out, the Muslim man became very animated and said, "What's that book? What are you reading? Why are you reading that? What's that about?" So I began to explain the book was on counseling; a book to prepare all kinds of people-helpers to listen to and help people who were hurting.

He responded: "Well my university professor said I should talk with a psychologist." I had two reactions to that: Do I want to be sitting next to a person on an airplane whose professor has told him, he needs to talk to a psychologist? The other reaction was, "I am a psychologist, so maybe God is in this."

We began to talk and very quickly he shared some of the personal problems that he had in his own life. We talked and swapped emails and I said that I would help him find somebody to talk to in Johannesburg. The reason I recount this story relates to the phrase "counseling as mission." Christian counseling needs to be open not only to Christians, but to opportunities to be a witness to people around the world who are yearning for some kind of help. Now I'm not saying that we evangelize in the name of counseling. There are ethical limitations in doing that. But there is a connection and there is a way in which we show people the love of Christ in our deeds, if not in our words, as we address counseling needs.

The 3 circle paradigm. In Reading, we also developed this 3-circle diagram.

* Smith, Collins, & Gingrich (2007)

The "egg yolk" in this paradigm represents the care of missionaries and humanitarian workers. This kind of work addresses about 400,000 people in the world, often highly stressed people whom we want to take care of due to the important work that they are doing for the Gospel in difficult places around the world. That is one part of care and counsel as mission. Harry Hoffman, who is here at this conference, is one of many people working in this area of member care. Based in Asia, he coordinates the World Evangelical Alliance's Global Member Care Network (GMCN) (www.global member-care.com). I thank God for the networks, the books, and the ongoing work that is going on in mobilizing this ministry to missionaries.

The next larger circle represents the ministry of the Christian church around the world. This circle represents about 2.2 billion people. The largest circle indicates the rest of the world, perhaps 4.8 billion people for whom Christ died and who need the Gospel.

Out of this small summit in Reading, MA came these conceptualizations which we realize are ambitious and quite difficult in terms of broadening and implementing our care for the world as Christians. After the meeting, Gary Collins wrote about it, and said:

> "Working in the big circle is difficult and complicated theologically, culturally, and clinically. It is work that is not well understood and may be controversial. Perhaps that is why it is the circle that is talked about the least. It is the "counseling as missions" circle where few have dared to go but where a growing generation of younger counselors appears eager to penetrate. We are discovering that there is a younger generation who get the connection between missions and counseling and in academic programs in the US they are wanting to somehow combine both of those efforts—counseling and mission." (personal communication)

Dr. Fred Gingrich and I are currently working on a book for Intervarsity Press entitled *Global Mental Health: Expanding the Church's Transforming Mission,* in which we are trying to capture and develop these ideas.

"Care & Counsel" in the context of poverty. The next city following Reading was Budapest in August 2007. At that time there was a Lausanne meeting whose official purpose was to launch the vision for the congress that was going to be held in Cape Town in 2010. It was at that meeting that Lausanne made official my role as the Lausanne Senior Associate for Care and Counsel. So the Lausanne partnership in this was launched at that time.

In addition to that, I met a man I hadn't seen for 20 years with whom I had worked closely at World Vision, a man from Mexico named Saúl Cruz-Ramos. Saúl went to be with the Lord in 2015, a great loss to the global church and this movement. Saúl Cruz was a man who lived with the poor, along with the whole Cruz family. They are a family of psychologists and mental health workers who work closely with the poor and have a deep understanding of transformational ministry. In Budapest, Saúl Cruz said to me

"Brad, you must pursue this." He went on to offer to host a consultation in Mexico City in Jan. 2009.

So we move on from Budapest to Mexico City where we held a consultation on "Care and Counsel as Mission" in the very poor city of Mexico City hosted by the Cruz family's organization Armonía Ministry (www.armoniamx.org; Armonía, a Spanish word, is similar to the biblical word "shalom").

This was a relatively small group of 22 people from 12 countries who gathered together for four days. Below is the consultation picture. Gary Collins (back row, third from the right) attended. Saúl Cruz-Ramos is on the left standing behind his wife, Pilar, and their daughter, Eidi; their son Saúl Cruz-Valdivieso is kneeling at the front right. Dr. Gladys Mwiti (a Kenyan psychologist) is in the middle row, second from the right. She and Dr. Al Dueck (far right) have co-authored a book on African indigenous Christian counseling (2006). Brad Smith is standing in the back row beneath the word "counsel".

Saúl Cruz, our host, had so many abilities and among them is that he was very clever. Many of us who had not lived in poor contexts were not familiar with large urban poor cities. So from the moment we landed at the airport, every part of that stop and go drive in heavy traffic across Mexico City was a teaching moment in which he shared with us regarding what it means to live and work among the poor.

The Cruz' hospitality and the places we visited where Armonía was working impacted our discussions about care and counsel as mission. This was not your everyday meeting of Christian counselors. As we talked about holistic transformation, the transformation of people in their bodies, minds, and spirits in the context of relationship and community, the observations and ideas that emerged were unique and challenging. We talked about poverty of all kinds and grappled with the spiritual dimensions of people's lives along with the sense of poverty beyond economic poverty.

We talked about indigenous Christian approaches, the fact that we can look at cultures and see how God has already given holy wisdom to people in all cultures, resources for them to help one another. We acknowledged and wrestled with the idea that we do not necessarily have to import from the West frameworks for helping people since there are resources already present in cultures that Christians can discover that could be helpful.

We talked about the relationship of evangelism to a holistic and integral mission. We also discussed our degree of commitment and resources for taking these days of rich dialogue and experience and developing ministries and partnerships to impact our particular locations. All of this was done to prepare for the next city which was Cape Town in 2010, the 3rd Lausanne global congress of about 5000 people.

Cape Town and the Declaration. The first "Lausanne" congress, called together by Dr. Billy Graham, was in Lausanne, Switzerland in 1974. The second was in Manila in 1989. These are special events that only occur every 15 or 20 years. Cape Town was the first of the congresses in over 40 years where Christian counselors were intentionally invited and included to meet with all varieties of people from the worldwide Christian church that were interested in world evangelization. There was a strong response to the Care and Counsel workshops and there was a special day-long tour away from the congress venue hosted by the Care and Counsel group. This was the most popular tour and it took us to an HIV/AIDS multifaceted holistic ministry called *Living Hope*, a ministry operated by a relatively small church, King of Kings Baptist Church in Fish Hoek, South Africa (www.livinghope.co.za). The themes of their ministry are Living Care (health care), Living Grace (homelessness & addiction), Living Right (HIV/AIDS education & prevention), and Living Way (economic empowerment). There was great interest in this kind of interdisciplinary work.

Emerging from this congress was the *Cape Town Declaration on Care and Counsel as Mission* (Smith, et al., 2011). It was written by a drafting committee of 12 people. The declaration has four major sections: Christian, holistic and systemic, indigenous, and collaborative.

Christian. The *Cape Town Declaration* affirms our commitment to the global Christian church by following Jesus in serving all people worldwide. The first distinction is that we do not only help Christians but we serve all people worldwide in order that they may flourish in every way. We believe it is a matter of biblical justice that resources and initiatives which meet basic human needs and promotes psychological wellbeing should be distributed equitably around the world.

This is something new that we do not hear a lot about from Christian counselors. As Christian counselors and helpers we are to be involved in justice issues as well as counseling. The work we do, the ministry we do, the things we have a passion for, are not just the things that happen one-on-one in the counseling room, even though that kind of work is very dear to my heart. But there is also a broader social responsibility that we need to be concerned about in terms of justice.

To illustrate this point is a rather disturbing video (Human Rights Watch, 2012). This video is from the country of Ghana and I'm grateful to say this video clip is a number of years old. It describes a troubling practice born out of the desperation of families not knowing how to respond to people with serious forms of mental illness. It describes prayer camps where mentally ill people are taken, often chained, and prayed for by pastors who have limited understanding and limited resources to help.

Ghana, along with many other countries, is trying to address these issues and governments are channeling increased resources into the care of the seriously mentally ill. However, this section of the *Declaration* says that an authentically Christian perspective on psychological care will call us to compassion, to seek justice, and to work toward reconciliation by our advocacy, practice, training and research. This is a new, broader understanding of all that is involved in Christian counseling that is focused on and informed by a global perspective.

Holistic and systemic. God's creation reflects a design of holistic, or interdependent, systems. First, addressing the holistic aspect of this, Rene Padilla (2005), a Latin American theologian, who has been very active in the Lausanne Movement, wrote the following, defining what holistic mission is: "...holistic mission is mission oriented towards the satisfaction of basic human needs, including the need of God, but also the need of food, love, housing, clothes, physical and mental health, and a sense of human dignity" (p.16). This is a much more complete holistic perspective on the needs of people.

One of the things that has been said about mental health is that mental health has been the "hole in holistic mission" (adapted from Canning, Neal, Fine, & Meese, 2002). It has been the missing piece. Holistic practitioners who work in community development, for example, have not known how to integrate mental health work into this form of ministry, but thankfully that is changing.

The second aspect of this section of the Declaration, systems thinking, refers to the belief that God's creation reflects a design of interrelated systems, the individual, the family, the church, the community, the culture, the region, the world. Those who signed the *Cape Town Declaration* are committed to a global understanding of the whole person existing within relational systems each involving suffering and health.

By the way, part of the macro system, I believe, includes principalities and powers, angels and demons: "For our struggle is not against flesh and blood, but against the rulers, against the authorities, against the powers of this dark world and against the spiritual forces of evil in the heavenly realms" (Eph. 6:12). I believe that we as Christians need to grapple with the entire spiritual world as part of what can impact people, and what can also impact governments and societies. We need to look at all of the systems that impact human well-being.

Indigenous. Culture is core to personal identity and culture is core to God's plan for the world. Culture was not a result of the Fall. The *Cape Town Commitment* (Lausanne Movement, 2011), the major document that came out of the Lausanne congress said that ethnic diversity is the gift and plan of God and creation. It has been spoiled by human sin and pride, resulting in confusion, strife, violence and war among nations. However, ethnic diversity will be preserved in the new creation.

Read the biblical book of Revelation. When people from every nation, every tribe, every people and language will gather as the redeemed people of God, this suggests that there will be ethnicity in heaven. There will be all kinds of culture and food in heaven. There will be Sauerkraut. There will be curry. I believe that all of the wonderful dimensions and artifacts of culture—food, clothing, customs, music, art—that bring glory to God and that we so enjoy and celebrate, will be part of heaven.

Culture is a gift from God and like all things it has been affected by the Fall; yet it is a wonderful gift and includes amazing resources for people to help one another. Thus a fundamental task for indigenous Christian helpers is to discern and engage with how God is already at work in a culture and not to picture the culture as either a blank piece of paper that desperately needs an American with a PowerPoint presentation to set them straight, or a grouping of people from which the image of God has been entirely erased.

Ethan Watters (2010), in his book entitled *Crazy Like Us: The Globalization of the American Psyche,* makes the case that Americans have exported their particular understanding of mental disorders leading to actually exporting the disorders themselves to other countries around the world. It is a fascinating book. Watters makes that case that there has been harm done to other cultures as we have not thought in culturally sensitive ways about mental health issues. Consider, for instance, the hundreds of helpers who landed in Sri Lanka after the tsunami and brought with them their own culture-bound definitions of trauma and their own checklists of how to assess people's trauma responses designed in the elite research universities in the U.S. At times these resources completely ignored the important questions to ask about how we can come alongside people. What have they learned? What has God shown them about how to survive and eventually thrive through a trauma like this? So often we skip right over those essential questions.

Collaboration. This concept includes a commitment to worldwide mutual empowerment. This is a different model than the exportation model where we in the West bring our expertise and dispense it within a different culture. This is a model where we genuinely care, listen and believe that we need to learn from one another because God is speaking to all of us in different ways.

In addition to this kind of collaboration among the helpers, there is another level of collaboration which involves a collaboration of mutual learning, mutual encouragement, and the journey towards wholeness that occurs between those who we are helping and we as helpers. Help is bi-directional, as they also help us. This bi-directionality of transformative relationships is something we saw modeled when we visited Saúl and Pilar Cruz and the transformation centers of Armonía Ministries in Mexico City where the model was that we all learn together. We learn from one another. In such collaborative relationships, the sense of power or hierarchy is minimized and there is a sense of mutual empowerment with God in the midst of it all.

Reflections on Care and Counsel and the Declaration

Those are the four major sections of the *Cape Town Declaration* and what I think would be helpful is for conversations to occur regarding these four points and for all of us interested in these issues to ask ourselves the question, what resonates with you about these four ideas? We need to interact with others, from diverse cultures and ministries, to talk with one another and listen and hear what resonates with each other about this, what excites you, what you see is important, and what you disagree with?

Comment 1: I'm not sure if this is fair but we found out that the bottom-line challenges in churches and communities across cultures, speaking globally, are the basic challenges in our Christian faith. For example, pride, forgiveness, humility. This is much more than ideology and this has been confirmed by the Bangladesh context, by the Jewish Palestinian context, and by the German context. So talking about holistic ministry, I'm personally observing that amongst the younger generation in Germany, they would rather have a holistic approach to live out their faith and not to do it so much in an apologetic way, like I was taught in the '80s. I'm referring to your quote about claiming that Jesus is the truth and that this must be demonstrated in deeds. This is important. It's a great opportunity. Of course, we believe the younger generation will have the same challenges with their own pride but it is a good way to go.

Comment 2: You're sharing your knowledge and you are sharing your PowerPoint, and that's collaborative and it doesn't seem like in the area of care and counsel that this is a practice that is well integrated in much of theological training. It's not really on the scope, at least if I think of places like Bangladesh, or of pastoral care in the church. I mean we've got cultural issues of talking about feelings, and about openly sharing, and about intruding in someone else's life. So these elements are really hard to overcome and to simply transfer Western concepts to solve. But on the whole it seems like there hasn't been a lot of collaboration. And I think we need to do more so. I appreciate that this is an open door and I think that it is an opportunity for us to take these ideas and go with it and move it on.

Comment 3: In our group, we talked about the three terms, holistic, indigenous and collaborative. We find this necessary, for example, in our work with other cultures. How do different cultures define mental illness? What are the reasons? How do they explain mental illness? How is, for example, the idea of person or selfhood defined in a different culture? Of course, this plays into the question of how we deal with mental illness. So we find that these terms, Christian, holistic, indigenous, and collaborative, are a very important part of dealing with these questions because we have to first understand and listen and find out how the other person, how a different culture, defines who the person is, how mental illness is understood, and how you can deal with it.

Comment 4: My name is Saúl Cruz-Valdivieso. I'm a part of the Care and Counsel as Mission group, and I'm also working with my mother in our ministry called Armonía. In our group we were talking about how the word "Christian" was very important in terms of counsel, and the term "indigenous." The reason is because sometimes we feel that in counseling or in therapy, we are pushed to forgive too soon and we are pushed not to acknowledge anger or fear or things like that. We are told that somehow they are wrong, when actually they are just natural things that are given to us by God, really I mean emotions.

We also talked about how indigenous is a very important word because it involves dignity. Indigenous brings us dignity in a way, or having an identity. And having an identity implies being responsible.

Comment 5: First, we really appreciate it that you emphasized that mental health has finally been recognized as being part of Christian mission. We as Germans realize that in German congregations there is little awareness about the nature of mental health and mental issues are still taboo. So we hope that this new way of thinking will lead us to really give mental health issues the proper attention in our congregations.

Comment 6: We talked about the indigenous piece and the importance of asking permission when we enter into another culture, asking about theology, asking instead of assuming, instead of bringing our own plan and determining what is important. We discussed the concept of working with cultures that really haven't split the concept of physical health from spiritual health, which we often have done in Western culture. That split is very tied together in some other cultures.

We asked ourselves how much is the issue of care and counsel really taught at seminaries, Bible schools and so on, especially in the Global South, and we expect that it's probably not very much. Maybe in a few places, yes, but there's lots of work to be done.

Comment 7: I am Harry Hoffman of the Global Member Care Network. I live in China. Missionaries usually come with a certain role and there is a whole industry of universities spreading out into the whole world and transporting the university systems and degrees into other countries. So there is no indigenous or collaborative effort but there is the selling of degrees. So the definition of counseling is even more important, what is counseling actually? Is it a university degree or is it just sitting together over a cup of tea?

Comment 8: (Dr. Smith) It is hard when you begin to shift within yourself and develop a new paradigm, trying as best you can not to be the

Westerner with all the answers, or the one that has the products to sell. In some ways, not to be too hard on the West but we have trained the rest of the world by all of our marketing to want at least some of what we have. I say this because sometimes I'm invited to speak in different places and I would love to be indigenous and collaborative and I would love to sit and say what have you learned? What is God showing you? What is it in your culture that God has really blessed you with so that for centuries you have found ways of living and often times thriving?

I would love to be collaborative like that and be indigenous and say "let's talk together. Let's pass the microphone around the room." But often I feel a pressure which is that when I offer that to people I get the response of "oh no, no, no, no, you're the American. We are competing with another school that has Americans and those Americans are giving them the secret knowledge that they can market. So that's what we want from you. Don't ask us questions. Don't focus on being collaborative. Give us the product." Even that is a process of understanding, discussion and trust building—of understanding the global dynamics as they are now.

Twelve Strategies for Care and Counsel As Mission

Following are 12 strategies for expanding the church's mission in the world by responding to mental illness. I will not be able to fully flesh out these points but I want to identify some challenges as we move forward in this undertaking, some issues that might cut across all of your ministry areas and are good to think about as we develop this new paradigm.

1. Reduce stigma. A really, really important issue in both Christian and secular contexts is the need to address the problem of stigma. This is the problem of shame and hiding. If you are working in a culture where there is tremendous shame about mental health issues, which seems to be every culture that I've discovered so far, even if you have a wonderful counseling center and resources available, there will often be an underutilization because of this issue of stigma.

One of the places to begin addressing this is by educating pastors. In my new context in Jackson, Mississippi about 75% of the churches are African-American. In an African-American church the pastor plays a huge role of influencer and gatekeeper. We are beginning a project in Jackson which will work to connect African-American churches with other mental health resources in the community. The message I've been given over and over again is the importance of influencing the pastors. You need to educate pastors. If pastors can be comfortable talking in the pulpit about issues having to do with mental health, they will likely be more supportive of other related efforts that might develop within the church. Educating pastors, church leaders, congregations and communities is a real cutting edge issue and will help reduce stigma in our churches and communities.

2. Integrate mental health into church health ministries. Many churches are developing health ministries and again my most recent exposure to this is with the African-American churches in the USA, but it is occurring in other places as well. If there is already a health ministry in the church perhaps screening and education around hypertension and diabetes and other common medical conditions, and connecting these issues to mental health resources is a way to integrate physical and mental health services.

In some cultures mental and physical conditions are so inextricably linked that needing to convince leaders of the mental health concerns is not necessary. However, in other cultures, it may be necessary to start with a broader health ministry and include mental health as part of that.

3. Advocacy for just allocation of resources for mental health at all levels. This first requires awareness of the data and of the needs in our own local and national contexts. Awareness of the resources or lack of resources and the need to build and rebuild programs and resources that are in jeopardy is essential. Advocacy, being a voice for those who have no voice, in the area of mental health is a Christian responsibility. All of the stigma, hiddenness and minimization of the importance of mental health often impacts our political leaders, as well, in terms of the prioritizing of government resources. Reminding them of the importance of these issues and educating them is important.

4. Use a comprehensive strategy that includes a continuum of care from education, prevention, screening, support services to group approaches and therapeutic interventions. Some of this looks like community psychology which is a smaller area of psychology, at least on the US scene. The fields of social work, public health, and nursing are very involved in this range of approaches and do not focus simply on traditional counseling and psychotherapeutic methods.

Oftentimes when counselors from the West speak and teach in international contexts they leave out this broader view of the continuum of care. Saddleback Church (www.sadddleback.com) in California is a huge church with many programs. Their "Signature Issues" include Celebrate Recovery (addition groups), HIV/AIDS support, PEACE Center (food, medical, legal aid, and resources), orphan care, Daniel Plan (physical disabilities), and Hope for Mental Health ministry. These are not traditional counseling ministries but are preventative and supportive services that many churches in different parts of the world do not have but could provide to some degree, not to replace counseling but to minimize the need for counseling because with more supportive services and education, there will not be such a need.

5. Offer services to the community as a witness to Christ. The Christian community development field has been aware of this tension between helping in the name of Jesus and being an explicit witness to Christ. Bryant Myers (1999), who wrote a book called *Walking with the Poor*, and development organizations in general , have wrestled with how can we be a witness? How can drilling a well in a village be a witness to Christ and to his love? The most important part of this is intentionally desiring to be a witness which is at the core of the Christian faith.

As counselors, how can we be a witness to Christ? The focus should not be on witnessing to the efficacy of short term cognitive behavioral therapy, even though this, like all good helping approaches, is a gift from God. All of the counseling techniques are gifts but how can what we do be a witness without evangelizing in a counseling session and witnessing inappropriately? Just being who we are, being known, and having the intention of sharing the good news of Christ, can be done in loving, caring, and ethical ways, both in word and deed.

6. Collaborate with other community groups and agencies. Collaborating with others in the community such as social service agencies, government services, and community groups is a part of being a witness. The goal is to build bridges and connections. Are there ways we can do a better job of working together? How can we refer to others, learn and teach others? Collaboration is central to how this new paradigm must operate.

7. Utilize task-shifting to increase resources by training laypeople and volunteers for appropriate work while providing supervision. There is a wonderful TED Talk on this concept of task-shifting by Vikram Patel (2012). The idea of task-shifting involves thinking strategically about things that people with a lower level of training, who when given sufficient training and supervision, can contribute significantly to care and counsel. There is some exciting research coming out of Asia and Africa on projects where, for example, primary health care workers who have a high school education are given a few weeks of training and are able to do effective counseling with mothers who are suffering from postpartum depression. With only a basic training program and supervision they are able to be effective helpers. The church in the West has long wrestled with the issue of lay helpers, elders and pastoral care providers and how to distinguish these ministry roles from professional counseling. We need to adapt these resources to mental health services within the church context. Obviously we need to be careful and use wisdom with this but there is an overwhelming need that requires us to shift our thinking from only professional service providers to tasks that others can do.

8. Address social factors impacting mental health like poverty and racism. Often, metaphorically speaking, the window shades of our counseling offices result in not seeing what is going on in the world outside. What is going on in the neighborhood and the world as we try to help people? Many social issues have a direct impact on counseling even if they are never talked about.

9. Include indigenous approaches to healing. This issue has been addressed earlier and contributes a central theme to this paradigm.

10. Consider using available technology integrated with personal contact. Considering the use of available technology which is integrated with personal contact is a rapidly growing component of mental health services globally. In many parts of the world, the internet can be helpful for supervision, for collaboration between counselors, and even some forms of counseling and psychoeducation. However, the Western assumption of high-speed internet and computers in every home and agency is not accurate. For instance my recent trip to Africa made me aware that are many places where there is very little internet. But, while internet may not be available, almost everybody has a cell phone. Phone apps are increasingly being leveraged to assist in mental health services. How could a cell phone be used responsibly, ethically, and helpfully for distance communication especially in underserved and isolated areas?

11. Broaden training for counselors to include program development, community approaches, and supervision. The training of mental health professionals needs to be broader than offering counseling services in traditional formats. Ideally, counselors, especially with higher levels of training, should be prepared not only for the task of doing counseling but be prepared as competent supervisors, to develop and operate programs, to write funding grants applications, and to incorporate community approaches.

12. Develop forums, networks, and partnerships for mutual learning and collaboration. Lastly, can there be networks, either online or in other ways that provide opportunities to learn from each other, collaborate with each other, and share resources rather than duplicating efforts, in the spirit of the Lausanne movement?

Concluding Comments

Given this list of 12 strategies, are there any issues that resonate with you and your ministry context? Are there strategies that you would like to add to this list?

Comment 1: I think mental health might be an excellent chance for churches to become partners with health systems. This is an ideal opportunity for churches to be appreciated by the government as we have something to offer in this regard.

Comment 2: What I'm missing is the term "inclusiveness" in the sense that if you look at those who struggle with mental illness where is the call of the church to advocate for their inclusion or integration into mainstream society as a normal part of society? Reducing stigma is fine, but what does this actually mean in a society where mental illness occurs?

Comment 3: By inclusiveness, I mean that people with mental health problems are a normal, accepted part of the mainstream of society. They are not excluded in any way, unlike how they are now. I mean accepting them as they are in society along with the deficits they have.

References

Canning, S. S., Neal, M. K., Fine, R., & Meese, K. J. (2002). Mental health resources: The "hole" in holistic, Christian, community-based health care? *Health and Development, 12*(4), 11–17.

Human Rights Watch. (2012, Oct. 16). *The case of prayer camps in Ghana.* Retrieved from www.youtube.com/watch?feature=player_detailpage&v=XHqdTUlcD4U.

Lausanne Movement. (2011). *The Cape Town commitment: A confession of faith and a call to action.* Peabody, MA: Hendrickson. Also available at www.lausanne.org/en/documents/ctcommitment.html#p1-7.

Lausanne Theology Working Group. (2007, Feb.). *Limuru Pointers: Following Jesus in our broken world.* Retrieved from www.lausanne.org/content/limuru-pointers.

Mwiti, G. K., & Dueck, A. (2006). *Christian counseling: An African indigenous perspective.* Pasadena, CA: Fuller Seminary Press.

Myers, B. (1999). *Walking with the poor.* Maryknoll, NY: Orbis.

National Institute of Mental Health. (2015). Retrieved from http://www.nimh.nih.gov/about/director/2015/mental-health-awareness-month-by-the-numbers.shtml.

Padilla, C. R. (2005). *Holistic Mission* (Lausanne Occasional Paper #33, Issue Group 4). The Lausanne Committee for World Evangelization. Retrieved from www.lausanne.org/wp-content/uploads/2007/06/LOP 33_IG4.pdf.

Patel, V. (2012). *Mental health for all by involving all* [TED Talk]. Retrieved from www.youtube.com/watch?v=yzm4gpAKrBk&feature=plcp.

Smith, B., Collins, G. R., Cruz, E., Cruz, P., Cruz, S., Cruz Jr., S., Dueck, A., Gingrich, F., Hughes, D., Mwiti, G., Vuncannon, J., & Warlow, J. (2011). *The Cape Town declaration on care and counsel as mission.* Retrieved from http://www.careandcounsel.org; www.belhaven.edu/careandcounsel/declaration.htm.

Watters, E. (2010). *Crazy like us: The globalization of the American psyche.* New York, NY: Free Press.

World Health Organization. (2011). Mental health atlas. Retrieved from www.who.int/mediacentre/multimedia/podcasts/2011/mental_health_17102011/en/.

World Health Organization. (2016). Mental health fact sheet. Retrieved from www.who.int/mediacentre/factsheets/fs369/en/.

Giving Voice to the Voiceless: Collaborative Inquiry in Poor Communities of Mexico City

Saúl Cruz-Valdivieso

Abstract

This article reports on a case study in the context of empowering persons in poor communities through a process of collaborative inquiry. This process began conceptually in the south of Mexico, and continued 28 years later in poor neighborhoods of Mexico City. This process of developing successful answers by communities for their well being was considered from indigenous (Mexican), holistic, Christian, collaborative and transformational perspectives. The communal discernment of members of communities in different contexts is reported as they were able to articulate for themselves the nature of psychological, relational, and spiritual well-being. This process of collaborative inquiry dramatically transformed the participants as they continued to cope with extremely difficult living conditions.

Introduction

This essay[1] will address a fundamental issue: "Does our limited analysis of the dimensions of poverty limit the way we seek solutions?" Harris, Nutbeam, and Sainsbury (2001) believe that poverty and other forms of social disadvantage are multidimensional in their manifestations, multifactorial in their causes, and complex in the way they operate on health and wellness. The purpose of this essay is to report on a case study of empowering persons in poor communities through a process of collaborative inquiry. This process began conceptually in Oaxaca, in the south of Mexico, and continued 28 years later in poor neighborhoods of Mexico City. This process of developing successful answers by communities for their well being is considered from indigenous (Mexican), holistic, Christian, collaborative and transformational perspectives.

---

[1] An earlier version of this article has appeared in the *Journal of Psychology & Theology*, 39 (3) Fall 2011, 222–232. The paper was originally coauthored by the late Saúl Cruz-Ramos and his son Saúl Cruz-Valdivieso.

In Voices of the Poor (Narayan, Patel, Schafft, Rademacher, & Koch-Shulte, 2000) there are personal and detailed stories of more than 60,000 men and women from 60 countries about the reality of living in poverty. For them, poverty is much more than an economic issue, poverty is not having a voice to influence the key decisions that affect their lives and speak to provincial and national political realities. We will argue that empowering the poor involves the creation of community that takes seriously indigenous thought forms and habits, is holistic in its approach to needs, builds on Christian convictions, and creates the space necessary for communal discernment.

Community Psychology in Latin America and Mexico

During the second half of the twentieth century and the beginning of the twenty first, Brazil, Colombia, Chile, Mexico, Puerto Rico and Venezuela have been the sites where intense development of Community Psychology (CP), both as a practice and as an academic subject, has taken place. CP in Latin America (LA) has been committed to and focused on solving social issues and problems. It has sought ways of understanding and action that are relevant to the social, economic, and cultural contexts of LA. Since its origins in the 1970s in South America, the academic approach of CP in Latin America, was first a form of psychosocial intervention geared to social change and only later integrated empirical practice with theory, a process they called praxis. Contrary to what happened in other areas of psychology in LA, CP did not just follow models and ways of thinking and acting constructed in other parts of the world. This conceptual and practical independence led to different models and forms of praxis, going beyond the contemporary emphasis on welfare assistance, the predominance of the mental health movement, and the dominant clinical-medical paradigm (Montero, 1998).

In the years before the 1970s there was a proto-social psychology phase when perspectives were ideological and used to justify authoritarian regimes, migration policies, and the creation of a submissive social conscience and identity. In the late 1950s and early 1960s there emerged a systematic affirmation of social psychology as a science, as a legitimate field for teaching and research. In the decade after the mid 1960s, social psychology went into a phase that consolidated it as an academic discipline but which was characterized by the non-critical reproduction of knowledge obtained outside Latin America, by a lack of contextualization and by the adoption of the experimental paradigm. As a result, it entered a crisis when the relevance of its teaching, research, theories, and methods were put into question. For the first time social psychologists were challenged and as a result Latin American practitioners and academics decided to write their own books. Not without its problems and limitations, these attempts gradually created a more sociological social psychology. It was after 1983 when the most advanced LA thinking entered into a phase of autonomous production of knowledge in terms of its relevance to problems emerging from LA's social reality and self-critical use of existing theories and methods. A distinctive feature of this phase is that CP had become a self-critical social psychology that revised itself, its goals, its foundations and its effects, either from a Marxist perspective or other philosophical points of view. The social foundations and theoretical frames of reference can be recognized in the work of Durkheim, Marx, dependence theory, and Freire, among others (Montero, 2003, 2008).

Theology of Liberation

Theology of Liberation (TL) became a major influence, acknowledged by the 1980s, in the area of community work and in the development of the concepts that have given shape to Community Psychology in Latin America (Montero and Varas Diaz, 2007). The origins of TL are in the First Latin American Episcopal Conference (CELAM), held in 1955 in Brazil where it was possible to open the way for conscientization of the bishops with respect to Latin American reality. Considering community as the place where freedom can be achieved, they analyzed justice and poverty. The Second Ecumenical Vatican Council organized by Latin American bishops and several other CELAMs followed. The interpretations of the priests manifested in these reunions were influenced by the conditions of underdevelopment, oppression, and exclusion suffered by large sectors of the Latin America population. The so called Eastern experience is the basis for the concept of liberation as a movement toward a deep social and individual conversion that leads to the structural change that is linked to the life saving action of Christ, to his death and his resurrection. Flores-Osorio (2009) considers that TL coincides with Paulo Freire (2002), seeking for the conscientization of the oppressed, while affirming the responsibility of catholic priests to build a world of freedom and dignity in solidarity.

A psychology of liberation was proposed by Martín-Baró between the 1960s and the mid 1980s. Liberation from this perspective "...is a process entailing a social rupture of transformation both the conditions of inequality and oppression and the institutions and practices producing them" (Montero & Sonn, 2009, p.1). Montero argues that liberation has a collective nature but that its effects also transform the individual, that liberation is a political process since it starts raising the awareness (conscientization) of the participants, that is, becoming aware of their rights and duties within their society.

Collaborative Inquiry

Socio-constructionism or social constructionism refers to a movement or a form of inquiry seeking to explain the processes through which persons describe, explain and make sense of the world in which they live, including themselves. From this point of view, knowledge is a construction and not a mental representation of reality. It considers that that the mind is relational and that the development of meanings is dialogical in nature. This stance, therefore, emphasizes the interactive and communal context as the creation of meaning. Social constructionism moves beyond social contextualization of behavior and simple relativity. It considers that the context is a multirelational and a linguistic domain in which behavior, emotions, feelings, understandings, among others, are communal constructions. These constructions or meaning generations occur within a plurality of networks of relationships and social processes are always changing, complex and within rich local discourses (Anderson, 1997, 2007; Berger & Luckmann, 1968, Freedman & Combs, 1966; Gehart, Tarragona & Bava, 2007; Gergen, 1985, 1996, 1997).

Collaborative Inquiry (CI), among other collaborative resources, has the potential of giving voice to the poor. According to Bray, Lee, Smith, & Yorks (2000), CI is an important way of conducting research into human experience for social scientists. It is a process consistent with how people learn in social contexts. It removes the separation of researcher from subject but perhaps more importantly, "it is a practice of fostering learning that denies that research is a form of learning reserved for specialists" (p.27). Kakabadse, Kakabadse, & Kalu (2007) suggest that fundamental to CI is the quality and degree of the inquirer's ability to be self-reflexive as they examine reality. This is of critical importance to the inquiry process and its internal validity. In a similar way, we use a reflective process to adjust and refine our practice since Schön and other theoreticians consider that reflexivity consists both of reflection-in-action and reflection-on-action. The latter is a posteriori activity that requires looking back on the process of experience. The former is live or happening in real time as an immediate activity that requires a catching-up learning action.

CI offers two advantages. On the one hand, it has been used as a social developmental tool (Gehart, Tarragona & Bava, 2007). CI as a tool allows for the co-creation of group knowledge and change through learning. Due to its philosophical position, it involves both the experiencing person and the persons conducting the research. In contrast to other action-based approaches, CI is concerned with human flourishing, whereby the participants occupy the dual role of co-inquirer and are the object of inquiry (Kakabadse, Kakabadse, & Kalu, 2007). From this interpretative perspective, the researcher is not outside of the inquiry process, but becomes a dynamic participant that shapes and is shaped by the process. The paradigm of CI is participatory and that makes engagement with the community critical (Anderson & Gehart, 2007; Gehart, Tarragona & Bava, 2007).

When considering the other strength of CI, Kakabadse, Kakabadse, and Kalu (2007) propose that the process leads to the co-creation of group knowledge and change through learning. Since the main resource of CI is the group, the group itself gives the primary interpretations of that it experiences. Ultimately the hermeneutic used is not a hermeneutic that is external to the group. The group and its local history are the appropriate interpretative horizon.

Armonía

It is in continuity with the above description of community psychology in Latin American that we established an association of communities called Organización Armonía, A. C. México. Mexico is a country where exorbitant wealth exists alongside unspeakable poverty. Many people still believe that poverty is simply a condition in which people lack basic resources. But poverty is really a culture, a way of life that affects every aspect of a person and their community. It is characterized by isolation, exploitation, helplessness, lack of vision for the future, and hopelessness (Aguilar-Monteverde, Carmona, Crestani, Mariño, Martínez, Palacios, & Paz-Sánchez, 2002).

For over twenty-five years, Armonía has been seeking to bring hope and transformation into this context. Armonía is developing a vision for a transformative role and a caring ministry by a team of psychologists/counselors and other professionals who work alongside disadvantaged communities. It began as our family ministry in the surrounding market areas of Oaxaca City in 1982 and is now an international movement of concern for the poor. By 1988 Armonía began to provide community psychology services as a nonprofit organization in the slums of Mexico City. This second stage was initiated when we as a family began befriending people in Jalalpa, (a slum area of Mexico City) walking alongside them, getting to know them, understanding the needs of the community, and encountering them in daily life. This led to the successive foundation of three Christian transformation centers in slum communities. By 1996, we also began to encounter problems in indigenous villages and in young indigenous students in rural villages in the state of Oaxaca, and we began to seek ways to improve their educational opportunities and to empower local inhabitants in their personal, relational and collective efforts to transform their lives for the better. Armonía works through the formation of local leaders who learn to solve their needs through our programs, counseling and systems of intervention. Armonía also promotes holistic community health, psychological counseling, prevention programs of children at risk, community transformation, vaccination campaigns for both humans and pets, housing improvement, emergency help, and the support of values that enhance the life of the communities from a Christian perspective.

At a community level, we seek to: (1) mobilize local and international communities to work together and reconstruct the whole quality of the life of the poor; (2) facilitate and participate in processes where we, together with poor communities can learn to respond as living communities to their present and future needs; (3) advocate for, and defend the rights of, the needy and the oppressed, learning to practice acts of justice and mercy in our daily relationships and; (4) reduce the vulnerability of the local communities and share Christian perspectives on the management of threats or the consequences of natural and human disasters and emergencies.

Together with helpers from the community began a treatment model that attempted to address the larger scope of the problems the families and communities were facing. We used little individual therapy and instead we emphasized meeting with families and groups of people from the community facing a problem. Over time the common problem would solidify the group, which transformed them into a community with a common goal where the members began to help one another. To our surprise, people with greater financial resources and education (doctors, priests, pastors, missionaries, school teachers, professors, accountants, lawyers and other professionals) began to attend our programs and reported that they or their relatives also suffered from common psychosocial problems. Soon an organizational and collaborative process took place in the psychology consultation office in which twenty-five couples or groups of families participated.

A supportive environment was created where participation of all of the attendees was encouraged through the narration of their personal stories, their sufferings, their failures, and their own solutions. Those solutions that seemed appropriate to the group and the psychologist would be included and publicly recognized as part of the repertoire of strategies for the group. The psychological team would take the material and, together with the group, would reflect on the problems and ponder the possible solutions, which now were collective and increasingly collaborative. Possible solutions to the problems would be reflected back to the families. On some occasions, it was necessary that parents and the psychologist would critically reflect on the cultural or traditional solutions that actually exacerbated the problem. The meaning of collective work and the group's communal resources were always the basis for possible personal solutions.

Without realizing it, the community members had begun to create a process of collaborative inquiry since clients were encouraged to look for broader support networks in government, civil, and religious institutions that could support long-term solutions. As well through dialogue with family members, or with people with similar problems, they found some of the solutions they needed. A clear example of the success of the Armonía approach is the Helen Keller School in Oaxaca City for children and young people with special education needs. This school was formed from collaborative inquiry and was directed by parents in an autonomous and local manner. Today it is self-supported by the older alumni's work who began attending as children by making fruit candy in their own factory with parents in charge of the commercial venture. Twenty-seven years after this project was started, the school now has it's own building, training and production workshops, administration rooms and auditorium, all run by the children's parents.

In 1987 my parents (Saúl Cruz-Ramos and Pilar Cruz) moved with our family close to the Jalalpa area in the West of Mexico City deciding to live temporarily near the neighborhoods where we thought we could facilitate poor communities organizing. Our community work here resulted, however, in the transformation of the trash dump, which we cleaned with locals over three years, into an Urban Transformation Center (UTC), relief work, and a construction program that built 87 houses for the sick and the poorest. After addressing the community's immediate problems of violence and natural disaster, we helped create new programs geared to protect children at risk, and to improve health and education. During those nine years, we developed an infrastructure to operate and we mobilized a network of volunteers and supporters from Mexico City and around the world.

Indigeneity: The Mexican Context

Maintaining a self-critical stance since the early years of Armonía, we accumulated questions and concerns about the nature of professional practice of psychology in settings of poverty. We believed a genuine concern with local community priorities and concerns was the critical element in our communication with the indigenous poor. That demanded an intense investment of time and resources in others, rather than in constructing our own edifice and responding primarily to our organizational needs (Cruz-Ramos & Cruz, 2002). We considered it necessary to construct an indigenous and contextually relevant perspective of community psychology, community intervention, and counseling that was Mexican and locally appropriate, rather than simply practicing or replicating Western approaches which formed the core of training in a Mexican university. As an example, Western experimental psychology gives less importance to field studies, and has historically defined the characteristics of the person conceptually and operationally without reference to the environment. That type of Western research seems to suppose that individual characteristics are the same regardless of the culture, social class, or the setting in which they are observed or in which the person lives (Bronfenbrenner, 2005).

In our involvement with the poor in Mexico City we had to learn that the extremely poor could not make sense of our initiatives in spite of our modeling and hence local adults would not collaborate. Their frustration showed us that a successful methodology in a one context cannot be imported into a new one simply by applying the same procedure. We also learned that even when the extremely poor live in a very crowded area, they feel isolated, fear each other, and see collaboration as dangerous. People in the slums where we were now working, did not have a sense of community. They just bumped into each other when they attended the Jalalpa UTC and we were just their friends outside their limited cardboard shacks and their relatives.

Holistic

A view of life built on individualism, functionalism, and scientism makes people think that holistic means total, that is, the result of a process of adding. According to Bronfenbrenner (2005), the term synergism is used to describe a phenomenon when "the joint operation of two or more forces produces an effect that is greater than the sum of the individual effects" (p.117). We need a more eco-biological-spiritual view of holism that would be more organic and more developmental.

In our work with the poor, we utilize a holistic (*integral* in Latin American Spanish) perspective. This has meant adopting an ecological metaphor based on Bronfenbrenner's work (1979, 2005) to create our theoretical framework and to develop a focus on the application of science in the service of social change and the improvement of quality of life for those in need (Castellá-Sarriera, 2008; Montero, 2003; Nelson & Prilleltensky, 2010; Prilleltensky, 2008). This approach brings together the answers provided from the domain of psychology and those provided by the domain of justice as necessary components for wellness. From a holistic perspective, wellness is the result of a synergistic relationship that is produced when personal, relational and collective needs are satisfied in a balanced way (Prilleltensky, 2008).

Christian

From a Latin American theological perspective, Armonía believes that a culture of poverty can be counteracted with the alternative culture of the kingdom of God, a culture in which compassion displaces force, love conquers fear, and poverty is transformed into life. Armonía endeavors to address the holistic culture of poverty with the whole gospel of Jesus Christ, a gospel that addresses the whole person within their whole society.

Integrating Christian faith and psychology is not so much a matter of application of theories, but the result of years of reflection-in-action (Schön, 1991) that finds a firm foundation in the Gospel's description of Jesus' feeling of compassion for the crowds, "because they were harassed and helpless, like sheep without a shepherd" (Mt. 9:36, NIV). Understanding the size, multifaceted nature and complexity of human suffering, brings clarity to the complexity and the importance of Jesus' holistic answer: "He went to them, teaching in their synagogues, preaching the good news of the Kingdom and healing every disease and sickness among the people" (Mt. 4:23–5:2; 9:35). Reading the context of Jesus' actions carefully, makes evident that he addressed the whole, suffering person in the towns and crowds, that is, he addressed the psychological, spiritual, physical, cultural, sociological and collective realms of people's lives. Jesus' response was holistic.

Transformational

Central among our concerns has been the emphasis on facilitating processes to resource poor communities to learn to take full responsibility for the solution of their problems. Taking responsibility for oneself and for others, however, needs to be preceded by a transformational learning process. This is best learned when the person is actually involved in constructing relationships of love and trust (Cruz-Ramos & Cruz, 2002).

Seeking transformation makes sense given the other perspectives from which we have chosen to see our psychological work among the poor. A concern to practice psychology that takes justice for the dispossessed seriously and empowers the needy implies, from a transformational perspective, participating alongside the poor, in actively resisting social, cultural and spiritual forces that distort and deform life in all its expressions. It involves learning to change the way we think by transforming frames of reference through dialogue and critical reflection on assumptions. Mezirow (1997) believes that to facilitate transformative learning, learners should be helped to become aware, critical of their own and others' assumptions, to recognize their frames of reference, to use their imagination to redefine problems from a different perspective, and to participate effectively in discourse.

Concern For Their Well being: A Case Study.

By the end of 2009 news of violence and crime, fear of financial chaos, lack of employment, the unexpected return to the country of those who had tried to find jobs in the US, the US financial crisis itself provoked a wave of anxiety in the whole country. Requests for counseling sessions grew in our community centers coming especially from younger adults whose children had been recently enrolled in our programs in our Urban Transformation Centers (UTCs). Contrasting with the turmoil, more experienced members of the UTCs were not concerned beyond what you would expect of those who live in a mega-city. Responding to the pressure of the newcomers, two leaders of the community centers in the west of the city requested funding for a full-time psychologist to address the critical situation. They argued that she could treat the cases of anxiety, depression and the like, originated by the situation. After consideration it was agreed to consult first with UTC members a possible way of action.

The co-directors had a conversation with Cruz-Valdivieso (who practiced in one of the west centers) visited Presidentes and Jalalpa UTCs, and spoke with groups of people in the UTCs. It became clear that it was necessary to encourage more conversations that would enable the communities to be in touch with their own resources. Our experience told us that they had answers about their own well being and that they themselves could find more solutions, dissolve many of the problems, learn how to help themselves through this situation, and create other realities.

Method

In January 2010, attendants, members, volunteers and employees of two Armonía Urban Transformation Centers (Jalalpa and Presidentes), were publicly invited by Cruz-Ramos to form a collaborative inquiry group for each center around the subject of psychological well being. In response to the invitation, in each of the two west centers a spontaneous group (which included around 12 adults who were local volunteers, members, attendants and employees) was formed. The average attendance for the total number of sessions was of six for Presidentes UTC and 10 for Jalalpa UTC. For Presidentes, one of the six was male and for Jalalpa, 2 were male. Participants ranged from 19 to 75 years of age, the average age for Presidentes was 45 and for Jalalpa 51. All had lived at least the last three years in the neighborhoods. Neither gender, marital status, number of children, political affiliation, religion nor level of education were conditions of participation. Although some of them had met before, in general they knew very little of each other. Their average level of education was of third year of primary education, although Jalalpa UTC group included a university student and two illiterate women.

The range of household income of all the attendants for both UTCs was between $15–120 US per week. The average weekly income for household for Presidentes was the equivalent of $50 US and $75 US for Jalalpa. One participant at Jalalpa was unemployed, while two were unemployed at Presidentes. The average number of children per household represented was 2.4 for Presidentes and 3.5 for Jalalpa. All participants of Presidentes had a couple while two were single at Jalapa and one was a widow.

There were five one-and-a-half-hour meetings at the Jalalpa UTC, and four two-hour at the Presidentes UTC. Their frequency was of one a week. After that number of sessions, the participants agreed that they were not obtaining any new information about psychological well being and the meetings were stopped.

The collaborative inquiry sessions took place at their UTCs buildings, located in very poor neighborhoods with a high concentration of people in the sector of Mexico City called Delegacion Alvaro Obregon. The average population concentration for Mexico City in year 2000 was 5,737 per square kilometer while it was 24% higher for this sector of the city. The deficit in available public space and basic services like markets, schools, medical clinics, hospitals, police stations, fire brigades, parks and transportation was in neighborhoods like Presidentes and Jalalpa and Presidentes 52% less in comparison with the rest of the city. Crime was high but there were no statistics available.

Procedure

At the beginning, the participants were instructed on how to be co-inquirers, how to engage in collaborative inquiry, how to generate their own questions, how to collaborate with others in the generation of ideas, how to initiate a question, and how to use the blackboard or other graphic materials. The sessions took place in a relaxed and open way where the researcher took on the role of a learner, rather than an expert (Anderson, 1997). The participants were also told that they themselves as researchers would interpret and seek practical and meaningful knowledge from experience. We approached the collaborative inquiry on psychological well being from the perspective of curiosity, attempting to stimulate dialogical conversations with all the members in each of the independent groups. As the original inquirer, Cruz-Ramos started the session by asking conversational questions that were informed both by what had been said and what had not yet been said. The purpose was to learn, explore, and clarify the group's input in a way that enhanced dialogue (Anderson & Goolishian, 1992). All sessions were audio recorded and some were video recorded with the agreement of the participants. All drawings and graphics elaborated for the study were kept for their collective analysis.

A follow-up session was held at each UTC one month after the inquiry had finished. To this session the general public in the neighborhoods was invited. The results were read and presented to the participants who had the freedom to correct, add, or disagree with what they were being presented. This session also had the purpose of disseminating the results of the inquiry for the common good.

The sessions

From the beginning the participants were active in developing conversations on the research theme, and every one contributed with his/her points of view, questions, answers, suggestions, sketches, drawings or even gestures and table games to the inquiry. In the sessions opinions and creative actions were very acknowledged and appreciated. Participants in the Jalapa UTC soon discovered that they were the real experts on their understanding of their own well being. These were issues in which they were the best informed, had the most authentic answers, and had the insider's perspective. It was clear that in the case of Jalalpa, elderly women had more influential voices and that they were willing to contradict each other. For example, tension developed within this group as one of the eldest participants suggested that well being is found when the members of a family do what they are told by the eldest woman in the house (which happened to be herself in her own family!). Another woman, who was ten years younger than her, challenged the idea. For this woman, well being was to be found when everyone and every couple in a household had their own mind and were able to participate in agreements of mutual benefit, not just to obey the eldest.

Others participated giving their opinions and engaging in dialogue as a group. Their dialogues were very friendly and they were accepting of their differences. In the first session the youngest participant at Jalalpa, stood up spontaneously, and began to write all the group's answers on a blackboard. After a while, another participant observed the coincidences and discrepancies and suggested a form to organize their ideas.

Since CI focuses on knowledge co-construction, both the CI leader and the participants participated in a process more of creation than one of recollection. That meant that we did not develop a frequency distribution of the participants' points of view. The differences were included as well. Soon the session became a generative process because the dialogue transformed or gave origin to new ideas, concepts and meanings that were not present before. After only a couple of meetings, it was evident that CI had formed a conversational society between the participants. In every group, people who started as practical strangers began sharing meanings and generate ideas together.

Once they had identified the factors and beliefs that gave them well being, the groups turned to the topic of their strengths, their capabilities, and the problem of being unable to maintain a reasonably constant state of high well being. They were able to identify the factors for their well being, but they didn't know how to construct a state of more stable personal and relational well being. At Presidentes, some of the participants created conceptual maps through drawings on what it meant to struggle to obtain an adequate level of well being in life. Others suggested telling stories about their strengths, weaknesses, failures and successes using a board game called "snakes and ladders." A snake square identified with negative situations while a ladder was identified with different stories in which they had identified their strengths and their resources to improve their well being.

At Jalalpa's UTC, some of the women cried when telling their stories of suffering, while the others comforted them. Some asked for explanations and others explained. The more influential women originally were the eldest. Once they knew each other's stories and the factors for well being had been identified by the group, the influence went to those participants who had some type of evidences of having persevered in achieving their well being such as having a good couple relationship, or having their grown up children in reasonably good employment or obtaining more education.

Outcomes

The participants analyzed their own themes in their conversations during the whole process of the inquiry. The interpretative process was continuous, and it was based on what was being said and what participants wanted to discuss. The following results were agreed upon by the participants themselves as a summary of results of their collaborative inquiry. 1) The factors whose satisfaction gave them personal, relational and collective well being, in order of importance, were: faith, family, service to others, a good relationship with the couple, good health, employment, being part of a group of real friends, and safety. The order varied between UTCs. 2) Most of them reported having high well being at a personal level, regular to bad well being at the relational level, and very low well being at the collective level. The latter mainly included security, employment, and salaries. None of them mentioned money spontaneously except in the form of salary level. 3) After some discussions at the Presidentes UTC, a differentiation between employment and work (as an activity where personal fulfillment is sought) was established by the participants. 4) Fear was considered a common state of mind that would not let them attend adult school, find a job, ask for a salary raise, go to the doctor, take therapy, speak with their spouses, live on their own, talk with their children or express their feelings.

Reflection-on-action

As mentioned in the method section, a public session was held in which the researchers presented the results to the participants in the CI. The two purposes of this meeting were verification and spreading the results of the inquiry for the common good. For verification of the analysis process, a recursive process of discussion was used in which the collaborators in the inquiry were asked to comment on, change, edit, add or challenge the conclusions that emerged from the research. In both cases, results were applauded and accepted with minor changes. The Jalapa meeting was well attended while at Presidentes the number of people was less than expected for reasons out of the control of the inquirers.

To share the results and conclusions of the inquiry on psychological well being with the larger groups for the common good, inquirers were invited to reflect on their actions and on the process that took them to discoveries and new knowledge. Reflections were shared by the participants themselves and included a great deal of emotion. New knowledge appeared in the midst of many tears, a change in attitude was manifest. The main area of change had to do with the problem of isolation and fear of collaborating by adults in extremely poor communities and the reflection-on-action was clearly identified. As a group of inquirers, they recognized publicly that in spite of their fears and lack of trust, they need each other to understand and practice their faith and their beliefs, to comfort and be comforted, to walk through transformation and to create new possibilities for relationships out of oppression.

One of them reported personal well being as she experienced a gradual withdrawal of fear from her life during the CI. She shared that she had decided to visit the doctor and accept her need for an operation on a brain tumor during the time of the sessions. She told the group how she had been helped to decide that it was worse to keep waiting than going for a solution that could bring well being into her life.

Some of them shared how the inquiry and corresponding dialogue within their group had helped them understand what was wrong with their personal and/or relational lives such as not establishing limits with their husbands or children, accepting violent relationships, or considering the male gender as superior. They also mentioned that the dialogue that started in the sessions had continued informally among several of them at the community center, on the streets and in their houses. In a general way, we can say that the groups adopted the method of reflection-in-action, and sometimes reflection-on-action, as their ways of working as groups of collaborators within their communities. Even when the research formally ended several of those who participated in the inquiry continued to get together regularly in their UTCs to discuss their needs, concerns, actions and resolutions.

Most of them agreed that they had discovered through the CI that their faith and their acts of love—that is, service to others—were the fundamental ways of maintaining their well being and communicating genuine care and commitment to the others so as to create new possibilities for transformation. At the Presidentes UTC, a former participant in the inquiry applied successfully for a job as an assistant in the UTC Day-Care program. At Jalalpa, two of them learned, from the others, how to set up successful boundaries in terms of how they were being treated by their husbands or relatives. It was also shared that a young and only daughter of one of the poorest inquirers of Jalalpa died in a heart operation just after the last CI session. People of Jalalpa had put together the money for the operation and now brought more resources for the burial. Their solidarity was uncommon. This woman who had lived most of her life isolated from the rest now had friends to bear her sorrow and to learn to walk without her daughter.

However, they also acknowledged that there was still the need to go further in inquiry about their collective needs and their responsibility to take action regarding peace, health, harmony, and justice at relational and collective levels. A commitment to maintain their conversational society was made and the others were invited to join them, as several critical topics had come out from the application of CI. They also decided to spread the news through conversations with other members of the neighborhoods who did not attend the UTCs but used the same market, school, laundry or were their direct neighbors.

Discussion

The outcome of the application of CI invites us into a triple celebration. The first relates directly to the change in meaning experienced by the communities linked to the UTCs as they were able and felt free to construct new perspectives on how to handle a specific threatening situation. This means that CI as a tool for research is effective in producing the answer to the questions the poor are asking. They were able to participate in an intersubjective process to articulate for themselves the nature of personal, relational (for the common good) and collective wellness.

The second reason for celebration relates to the fact that they co-constructed their knowledge having themselves and their stories and own meanings as their main resources. This is in itself a liberating and transforming experience that challenges the voices and powers that condemn the poor to a life of servitude without any recognition of their contributions.

Thirdly, we celebrate that we are allowed to understand the process that leads to the co-creation of group knowledge and change through learning as we seek to care for and serve the poor. In effect, mobilizing and organizing the poor into process of community creation and into processes of transformation could be one of the main sources of frustration in the field work. CI offers the possibility for both relevant knowledge and transformation but in the hands of the group and its local history.

We should acknowledge that at this point Armonía is part of a Latin American movement in community psychology not a product or result of it. In fact, until very recently there were no institutions where these themes could be studied. Even today, most of them offer only basic degrees and there are few examples of real insertion of academia into the social problems of this country. There are many common ideals and dreams shared with Freire's dialogical pedagogy, Martín-Baró's Psychology of Liberation, the Theology of Liberation, Montero's quest for an indigenous social psychology, Prilleltensky's concern for justice, Serrano's passion for gender equality, and many others. Even when their theoretical work and methods were developed in other countries, their influence through magazines and a few books in libraries were very powerful. We are thankful for their lives, their work and their sacrifices as many of them were the precursors of what today we are using in the communities where we work. It was probably our Protestant-Evangelical posture that kept us walking on separate paths because of our rejection of predominant ideas such as the polarization between the oppressor and the oppressed as the main hermeneutical key to understand our Christian responsibility. Perhaps it was our commitment to peace and to acts of peace that would not coincide with concepts of famous TL theologians on the "Just War", or the Marxist analysis of the biblical texts without letting the text interpret itself. It was also our stubbornness in developing our own experiences, our own integrations between psychology and theology, the development of our own theology and our own psychology as we felt it appropriate and relevant to our context. We felt the need to formulate our own ideas that kept us seeking for an ideological framework that responded in adequate and fluid ways to meet the need for more useful ways of conceptualizing, describing and working with human systems, the problems they present, and what we can do for them in a context of poverty. At the same time, we have argued above that practicing psychology in our Mexican context with disenfranchised poor populations, the role of the psychologist is that of a reflective practitioner and an active participant, in therapy, consultation, learning, teaching and research (Schön, 1991).

References

Aguilar-Monteverde, A., Carmona, F., Crestani, M., Mariño, A. I., Martínez, G., Palacios, I., Paz-Sánchez, F. (2002). *El México de hoy: Sus grandes problemas y qué hacer frente a ellos.* Zacatecas, México: Porrúa.

Anderson, H. (1997). *Conversations, Language and Possibilities.* New York, USA: Basic Books.

Anderson, H. (2007). A postmodern umbrella: Language and knowledge as relational and generative, and inherently transforming. In Anderson, H. & Gehart, D. (Eds.), *Collaborative therapy: Relationships and conversations that make a difference* (pp. 7–19). New York, USA: Routledge.

Anderson, H. & Goolishian, H. (1992). The client is the expert: A not knowing approach to therapy. In McNamee, S. & Gergen, K. J. (Eds.), *Therapy as Social Construction* (pp. 25–39). London, England: Sage.

Anderson, H. & Gehart, D. (Eds.). (2007). *Collaborative therapy: Relationships and conversations that make a difference.* New York, USA: Routledge.

Berger, P. & T. Luckmann. (1968). *La construcción social de la realidad.* Buenos Aires, Argentina: Amorrortu.

Bray, J. N., Lee, J., Smith, L. L., & Yorks, L. (2000). *Collaborative inquiry in practice.* London, England: Sage.

Bronfenbrenner, U. (1979). *The ecology of human development: Experiments by nature and design.* Cambridge, USA: Harvard University Press.

_____ (2005). Ecological systems theory. In U. Bronfenbrenner, (Ed.), *Making humans being human: Bioecological perspectives on human development.* (pp. 3–15). Thousand Oaks, USA: Sage Publications.

Castellá-Sarriera, J. (2008). El paradigma ecológico en la psicología comunitaria: del contexto a la complejidad. En Montero, M., *Introducción a la psicología comunitaria.* Buenos Aires, Argentina: Paidós.

Cruz-Ramos, S. & Cruz, P. (2002). Integral mission and the practitioner's perspective. In Chester, T. (Ed.), *Justice, mercy and humility: Integral mission and the poor.* (pp. 89–101) Exeter, England: Paternoster Press.

Freire, P. (1970). *Pedagogía de la esperanza.* Mexico City, Mexico: Siglo XXI.

Flores-Osorio, J. M. (2009). Praxis and Liberation in the Context of Latin American Theory. In Montero, M. & Sonn, C. C. (Eds.), *Psychology of Liberation: Theory and Applications.* New York: Springer. 11–36. doi: 10.1007/978-0-387-85784-8

Freedman, J., & Combs, G. (1996). *Narrative Terapy: The social construction of preferred realities.* New York, USA: W. W. Norton.

Gehart, D., Tarragona, M. & Bava, S. (2007). A collaborative approach to research and inquiry. In Anderson, H. & Gehart, D. (Eds.), *Collaborative therapy: Relationships and conversations that make a difference* (pp. 367–387). New York, USA: Routledge.

Gergen, K. J. (1985). The social constructionist movement in modern psychology. *American Psychologist,* 3, 40. Washington, DC, USA: American Psychological Association.

_____ (1996). *Realidades y relaciones: Aproximaciones a la construcción social.* Barcelona, España: Paidós.

_____ (1997). *El yo saturado: Dilemas de identidad en el mundo contemporáneo.* Barcelona, España: Paidós.

Harris, E., Nutbeam, D, & Sainsbury, P. (2001). Does our limited analysis of the dimensions of poverty limit the way we seek solutions? In Eckersley, R., Dixon, J., &Douglas, B. (Eds.), *The social origins of health and well-being* (pp. 259–268). Cambridge, United Kingdom: Cambridge University Press.

Kakabadse, N. K., Kakabadse, A. P. & Kalu, N. K. (2007). Communicative action through collaborative inquiry: Journey of a facilitating co-Inquirer. *Systemic Practice and Action Research* 20, 245–272.

Mezirow, J. (1997). Transformative Learning in Action: Insights from Practice. *New Directions in Adult and Continuing Education,* 74, 5–12.

Montero, M. (2008). *Introducción a la psicología comunitaria*. Buenos Aires, Argentina : Paidós.

_____ (2003). *Teoría y práctica de la psicología comunitaria. La tensión entre comunidad y sociedad*. Buenos Aires, Argentina: Paidós.

Montero, M. & Sonn, C. C. (2009). About liberation and psychology: An introduction. In Montero, M. & Sonn, C. C. (Eds.), *Psychology of Liberation: Theory and Applications* (pp. 1–10). New York, USA: Peace Psychology Book Series. doi: 10.1007/978-0-387-85784-8

Montero, M. & Varas Díaz, N. (2007). Latin American community psychology: Development, implications, and challenges within a social change agenda. En S. M. Reich, M. Riemer, I. Prilleltensky & M. Montero (Eds.), *International community psychology: History and theories* (pp. 63–98). New York, USA: Springer.

Narayan, D., Patel, R., Schafft, K., Rademacher, A., & Koch-Shulte, S. (2000). *Voices of the poor: Can anyone hear us?* Oxford, England: Oxford University Press for the World Bank.

Nelson, G. & Prilleltensky, I. (2010). *Community psychology: In pursuit of liberation and well-being*. New York, USA: Palgrave Macmillan.

Prilleltensky, I. (2008). Validez psicopolítica: El próximo reto para la psicología comunitaria. In M. Montero (Ed.) *Introducción a la psicología comunitaria.* (pp. 5–20) Buenos Aires, Argentina: Paidós.

Schön, D. (1991). *The reflective practitioner: Case studies in and on educational practice*. New York, USA: Teachers College Press.

Indigenous Christian Counseling in Africa:
The Call of the Church to Care and Counsel as Mission

Gladys K. Mwiti

Abstract

Christian Counselors are called to the ministry of compassion and comfort and so Christian counseling can be classified as mission. In 2.Cor. 1:3-7, Paul repeated the word "comfort" nine times in five verses. Christ, the Healer is with his Church, and his healing flows through empowering the Church to become a healing community. This reality gives us the confidence to equip lay counselors within the body of Christ. Today, we focus on Africa because the Continent is currently central with regard to global Christianity. Christianity is the fastest growing religion in the Continent, indicating that, at the moment global Christianity is centered in Africa. This does not mean that the North is losing out because wherever the Church grows, global Christianity grows. However, this growth poses a challenge in that the Christian focus and emphasis should be wherever the Church is growing fastest.

We need to recognize that, although the center of gravity of the global Church is shifting south, major resources of the Church are still in the North: the best equipped seminaries, the finest biblical historical libraries and the richest endowments committed to mission and clergy training. Therefore, as much as we celebrate these historical endowments in the North, there is need to consider the implications of the role of the global Church in sustaining the Church in the South especially in the role of care and counsel as mission. The growth and strength of the Church in the South is additively the growth and strength of the global Church. Projections suggest that in ten years' time, African Christians will form the largest continental block of the faith, outgrowing Europe and the Americas. These projections have unfathomable spiritual, historical and political significance because outcomes will change Christianity not only in Africa but Global Christianity as well. Care and counsel as mission needs to explore the role of mental wellness on individual and community resilience. What resources does the Church have in the mission of care and counsel? What models can the Church utilize to ensure that Christians are mobilized to care and counsel?

Introduction

In his book on current trends of global Christianity, Jenkins illuminates the remarkable expansion of Christianity in the global South: Africa, Asia, and Latin America (Jenkins 2011). He believes that the center of gravity of global Christianity is shifting from the North to the South. What is the role of the global Church in care and counsel as mission, with a focus on Africa? This responsibility is motivated by the call of Jesus Christ for the Church to be a caring community: rejoicing with those who rejoice and mourning with those who mourn (Rom. 12:15). Jesus desires that his followers live abundant lives (John 10:10) and learn to comfort one another with the comfort they receive from God.

Africa struggles with many factors that are linked to compromised mental wellness, indicating that care and counsel as mission will need to be holistic, addressing the needs of the body, mind, spirit, relationships and social-community challenges. There are indigenous resources in these networks that can be utilized towards restoration of wellness.

The implication is that care and counsel as mission needs to engage factors related to causes and outcomes of poverty, war and conflict, disease, oppression, radicalization, violent extremism and terrorism, corruption as well as stress, burnout and compassion fatigue. The Church of Christ can do more than preach solely about heaven because the reality is that people should live abundantly on the earth even as they wait for eternity. Many difficult challenges call for Care and Counsel as a mission of the Church in Africa. Among these are the devastating outcomes of the AIDS pandemic, the impact of poverty on mental health, the outcomes of war and conflict and the effects of violent extremism and terrorism, among others.

Bereavement and Loss

Africa has not adequately dealt with the multiplicity of death and loss as well as the emotional impact related to disasters like the AIDS pandemic. When parents and breadwinners die, the outcome is that the safety and health of children is compromised and community resiliency broken, leading to poverty and malnutrition (Keene Reder 2003). The tragedy of the AIDS pandemic in Africa is that often, interventions, even major ones funded by well-knowing international partners, omit emotional and psychosocial support in planning for HIV and AIDS programs for Africa. Top of such agenda is mother-child transmission, healthcare, economic development, education, and so on. This reality ignores the immensity of the mental health fallout of the AIDS pandemic when, for example, UNAIDS (2014) reports that in 2013 only, between 1.0 million and 1.3 million people died of AIDS-related causes. A dead person represents a brokenhearted family and a grieving community. In addition, every funeral implies use of resources for burial procedures, as well as care of orphaned children. Every community in majority of Africa has a Church, and well-equipped, Christians can continue to bring much-needed healing, hope, care and comfort to individuals and communities in mourning.

The Refugee Crisis

With a large Muslim population especially in North Africa and the global push for Islamization of the world by Muslim extremists, Africa has been affected by violent extremism and the outcomes have left some nations devastated. UNHCR (2015) reports that in the Central African Republic, since the anti-Balaka militia overran the capital Bangui in December 2013, there are already 425,000 refugees, most of them in Cameroon and southern Chad. These two nations are already receiving thousands of refugees from violence in North-Eastern Nigeria. In 2014, UNHCR and partners appealed for US$ 210 million to support basic life-saving initiatives. These would be mainly food, medical care and shelter. In addition, these masses have experienced psychological trauma, grief and loss leaving many broken and mentally challenged. In addition, they also have lost their nationhood, hope and meaning. Many arrive in rescue centers with stories of burnt villages, violence, murder and sexual violence. Others carry physical wounds and deeper pain of bereavement.

Some of the factors that contribute to Africa's refugee and migration problem are political oppression, poor economies and destruction of the environment. Conflicts and wars contribute to the largest bulk of displaced people (Akokpari 2002). The needs of displaced people call for global and local partnerships for pastoral care and counsel as a mission of the Church. Pastoral theology makes meaning when it is incorporated into cultures and concrete situations of the target population. As part of pastoral theology, pastoral care is inspired by Christ's redemptive concern for humankind and the call of Christians to become bearers of that message to a broken world (Mobie 2005).

Beyond becoming safe places for the alien, the most effective role of the Church is prevention of factors that create instability as well as teaching and modeling environmental stewardship. Churches in Sub-Saharan Africa may need to create proactive interventions for refugee ministries along with other departments of the Church. Environmental stewardship involves participation, partnerships, public policies and awareness-creation in the preservation of water and natural resources.

The Importance of African Indigenous Approaches

Africa has gone through *dismembering* (Mwiti & Dueck 2006). Over the decades, the Continent has been torn apart with destruction of her personality, values and nationhood. The Continent carries colonial legacies that have lived on, many of them in the form of decisions that impact her present and future made externally without consultation with beneficiaries. Most of the time, these decisions result in packaged solutions delivered without consulting the recipients. In the 1980s, for example, in the public sector of the Saharan nations there were over 100,000 donor-funded projects, but they engaged expert advisors who utilized more than 35% of the development assistance to the region although these regions would have provided this expert manpower locally (Kimenyi & Datta 2011). So the nations in this region would receive a grant and overseeing the grant were expatriate executives and professionals as if there were no local professionals to do the work. This amounts to top-down control that erodes indigenous problem and project ownership through devaluing indigenous professionalism.

Beyond devaluing indigenous resources, problem and policy analysis by local expertise was marginalized. There was non-inclusive decision-making in political and development initiatives and this was masked by similar struggles within the Church. Use of indigenous people and their resources in care and counsel as mission implies that indigenous people will finally have a voice in the care of their own people. Paternalism and non-inclusivity has colored global mission and church planting over many decades with the outcome that mission enterprises especially from the West "settle for a cultural version of Christianity that is far from the real thing" (Wilberforce 2006, 23–24), so comprising the relevance of the Gospel in its ability to utilize local resources in meeting felt needs. However, this is mainly becoming a historical fact Africans are taking charge of church planting and missions, creating inclusivity is new local and global partnerships.

It follows that use of indigenous resources in care and counsel as mission can encourage application of locally available assets in training and practice of psychology. This is because most counselors and psychologists working in Africa have been trained in Western non-African understanding of psychology and so need to enter communities not as experts but students of that particular population. Similarly, there is need for evidence-based and biblically-informed integration modalities in the training of Church-based mental health workers. From personal experience, in spite of my many years of work in Rwanda almost five years post-genocide engagement as Oasis Africa trained local indigenous trauma counselors for that nation, I am still in the process of understanding the genesis of the 1994 genocide, still a student of indigenous Rwanda.

Some years ago, a friend heard that I was in California when their ladies' group was scheduled to watch the movie *Hotel Rwanda*. They invited me to come and try to help them understand why the genocide in Rwanda happened. As a therapist, I try to be emotionally self-controlled but this day, as we watched *Hotel Rwanda*, something broke. In the scene where they evacuate United Nations expatriate staff from the Hôtel des Mille Collines, children sing a song in Kinya-Rwanda. During the melody and the scenes of the evacuation, I found myself weeping uncontrollably. Before my eyes played the helplessness of my people, and thoughts of millions of orphans in the continent was like a dark cloud washing over me. My hostess seated next to me patted me on the back and said: "Don't worry. Don't worry. It happens to all of us!" I am sure that she had no clue why I was weeping. At that moment, I felt that the pain and suffering of Africa was trivialized as the women kept on sipping their tea, making small comments and seeming totally disconnected from the horror of that genocide.

At the end of the film, they asked me to explain what happened in Rwanda. I stood up and all I said was: "Ladies, I don't know. I have no clue why the genocide happened." There is a possibility that many of these women were moved by the carnage in that documentary or that some disconnected from the realities of the genocide. I will never know. However, I am convinced that we shall be poor helpers if we are poor listeners and learners. Humility is the key to any learning.

Today, Rwanda is a blossoming nation that shares many indigenous factors that make Africa a resilient continent. Care and counsel helpers need to become students of that resiliency before we unleash theories of psychologists like Freud, Rogers or Maslow and other Western counseling approaches. Tested principles of Western psychology matter but counselors in Africa should desist from a cut and paste application versus integration.

Re-membering of Africa—Using African Resources for Care and Counsel

Although Africa has gone through decades of dismembering from colonialism to neo-colonialism, many of her nations are going through post-colonial transition, with a move towards liberalization, informed decision-making and development collaborations from regional to community levels. Years of oppression and poverty have given rise to depression, anger, and revenge. Sustainable re-membering of Africa will need to use the massive resources in the Continent. One of these is Africa's human capital. Africa is the only region of the world where the population is projected to keep increasing through the 25th century. At present there are 1.2 billion people, more than five times the population of 1950. By 2050, Africa's population will double to 2.4 billion eventually reaching 4.2 billion by the end of the century. This is just equal to the population of the world in 1977. There is also a projection (UNICEF 2014) that by 2050 about 40% of all global children will be in Africa for in the next 35 years, 1.8 billion babies will be born in Africa causing the Continent to double her population and its under-18 population will increase by two thirds to reach 1 billion. The implication is that Africa has, and will continue to have the human resources to grow many teams of helpers to bring healing to her own people.

Besides African human capital is the current rapid increase in technology and IT opportunities. In a 2014 report by GSMA, a global association of mobile service providers indicates that the mobile industry is driving explosive economic growth in sub-Saharan Africa. The region is the fastest growing area for both connections and unique subscribers. In 2014 there were six to eight million connections representing the highest proportion of mobile versus fixed line connections in the world. Kenya, for example, has 80% mobile telephone coverage (CAK 2014), and using the mobile money platform, more than $1.7 trillion passed through Kenyan mobile phones in 2013. The current forecast is that by the year 2020 sub-Saharan Africa, which makes the highest growth of any region in the number of smart phone connections, will have over half a billion mobile subscribers, contributing 5.4 per cent to Regional GDP. This growth accounts for more than half of the total globe connection base (GSMA 2014).

The mobile telephone growth provides unique opportunities as a gateway to essential services especially in health care (Bouverot 2014). Most of these mobile phones are smart phones, and many people, especially youth and young adults, already have their Bibles online on smart phones or iPads, as well as many apps like WhatsApp. How can the Christian community use mobile technology for care and counsel? Already, some teams are thinking of mobile apps for suicide prevention, psycho-education on stress management and depression, and so on. Currently, in their love for association, there are thousands of WhatsApp groups formed among friends, family, interest groups, security teams, and so on. The Kenyan government today is taking mobile services to the poor and the rural people using the mobile phone. There are farmers' apps, potato sellers' apps, and many more. Opportunities exist for the Church to create care and counsel apps to propagate the transforming healing messages of the gospel.

Africa has indigenous resources intertwined with her traditions, for example, proverbs that can inform thinking in counseling and therapy situations, as well as metaphors, folktales, and rites of passage that guide understanding of developmental stages and psychopathologies that result from delayed or interrupted development. We have dance, song and musical drums. For example, working with communities in trauma, the question would be: "When you experience loss and grief in your community, what do you do to heal?" Learning from the community would inform psychological and biblical approaches such that what the counselor or therapist provides is an integrated perspective that finds meaning and relevance in the lives of the recipients.

The Church is called to become a caring community within African indigenous communities that already have care for the vulnerable as shared value. Traditionally, care for orphans is ingrained in African communities. In my tribe, the Meru people of Kenya, for example, the word "orphan" does not exist because when parents die, immediately the community takes up the children. This resiliency is threatened by millions of orphans from the AIDS pandemic, but the Church can become the new community in care of the most vulnerable. Similarly, in many African communities, child protection was ingrained in community values. One of the methods was through child naming. For example, among the Meru of Kenya, the first born son is named after the father's father, even if the man is deceased. From the shared naming ceremony, the mother knows that she is taking care of her mother in law's husband, and that the older woman will be watching very carefully for any child abuse or neglect. Any such consistent careless behaviors were punishable by the mother-in-law's cohort of women age mates. This made child rearing a shared community initiative.

Rites of passage are indigenous values used to train young people how to cross over from childhood into adulthood, to become men and women. For both sexes, many communities had traditions of encouraging each cohort to move on to the next level of adult responsibility. This opportunity was full of teaching, training and mentoring, ensuring that all young people move on to the next level together. The cohort provided social support and mutual encouragement in the process of becoming men or women. Many African churches have borrowed the indigenous practice and integrated it into Church-based training for young people through the process of rites of passage. In my book on youth maturation (Mwiti 2005), I discuss the reality that currently among many African Christian parents, three critical activities go on in tandem when children enter adolescence. At age 13, the youth go through critical national school examinations that prepare them for competitive admission to high school. In this process, some parents are even more anxious than their children because poor examination results might mean missing a place in a good high school.

At the same time, at age 12 or 13, in many churches, the young people undergo several months of confirmation classes learning the Christian doctrine, culminating in confirmation and the first Holy Communion. At the same time, as they complete primary school in readiness for high school, that final December holiday, young men undergo circumcision and emerge as young adults ready for high school. In my book, I propose that the Church can coordinate these three parallel processes under trained lay counselors. The Church can partner with the school program as well as with parents within their communities to offer six-months training for adulthood where all these three major activities are done in a teacher-parent-pastor team co-ordinated by the Christian Counselor.

Beyond training youth for adulthood, every indigenous community had a way of training and preparing couples for marriage. Premarital counseling and marriage counseling remain critical ways in which the Church can engage the ministry of care and counsel. This is because already, weddings are shared community activities offering an automatic forum for ministry. Other types of care are in trauma ministry because disasters provide an opportunity for Christians to offer the compassion of Christ. Once again, caring for the less fortunate and the wounded is a mutually shared indigenous value because Africans are generous by nature. These and many other indigenous riches are available to be integrated into Church-based care and counsel ministries through creating a caring community of care givers with a rich Christian approach undergirded by indigenous cultural riches.

Social Support as a Value for Care and Counsel

Social support in Africa is another indigenous value the Church in Africa can use for care and counsel as mission. From time immemorial, the cooperative enterprise has been used for poverty eradication in Kenya and currently, the nation tops Africa in the use of microfinance, savings and credit cooperatives (Ndii 2004). Working in groups creates ownership, accountability and control for sales of products, farming, transport, fishing, microfinance, and so on. For example, motorcycles, called *boda bodas* are used as a mode of transportation, whizzing passengers through villages or busy streets. Some years ago, 100 boda boda operators started a microfinance enterprise or table banking each contributing 200 Kenyan shillings equivalent of $2 US every month. After several years, they took a loan from the bank to buy property. The young men acquired land, split it in parcels and constructed homes. Today each of them owns a two-bedroom apartment. Together they were able to do more. It is estimated that 63% of the Kenyan population directly participate in the cooperative movement and that 80% of Kenyans are deriving their income from the same. These gatherings provide an automatic forum for spreading the message of care and counsel.

The Oasis Africa Ripple Effect Model—Three Levels of Care and Counsel

The content of training of care and counsel counselors and psychologists should be informed by theology-enlightened psychology where seminaries not only add the subject to their curriculum but also develop theology surrounding critical questions like morality, marriage, the family, parenting, ethical leadership and so on. Mwiti & Dueck (2006) present an indigenously-sensitive and Christ-centered counseling and psychology approach. Out of this is the Oasis Africa three-legged African stool model that incorporates sound psychology, biblical theology, and the third part of indigenous cultural values. Training pastors in such models ensures that they graduate from seminary equipped in a holistic grassroots-oriented indigenously-sensitive counseling methodology. Within the Church, teams are created using a training of trainers' model where after graduating in the first level, Level 1 of Care and Counsel, trainers go back to their churches to train more counselors to offer services each at their level of lay or professional training. All the three levels described below go through Level 1 of training so that there is coherence, teamwork and mobilizing the Church towards taking up this ministry. They are also trained to use their gifts at whatever level because many Christians disconnect professional life from ministry in their churches.

Level 1 of the African stool model represents care, compassion and encouragement that Christians can offer by the virtue of their commitment to Jesus Christ. Trained in listening and basic counseling skills, Christian counselors can offer services similar to Psychological First Aid, a basic trauma counseling model where after listening and knowing people's needs, one can encourage the affected, build hope and then link them to resources. These are the services our organization, Oasis Africa, offered after the genocide in Rwanda and the 1998 USA Embassy bombing in Nairobi.

Level 2 people are program supervisors, many of them with a Bachelor's degree in counseling, theology, social work, education, or other professions where they are trained to work with people. These are people supervising others in children's homes, schools, hospitals, community projects, companies and government offices. They may be professionals in their own fields of teaching, education, social work and so on but are paraprofessionals in counseling. Additional care and counsel skills will enhance their ability to coordinate helping programs in their domains.

For Level 3, we partner with professionals in counseling or psychology who have a Masters or Doctoral degree to offer supervision, mentoring and coaching. These individuals are in our churches and communities and can serve the Church in supporting the care and counsel team. This team receives support from their places of work: clinics, hospitals and schools, where their supervisors ensure ethical practice and as well as professional growth through continuing education training.

Sensitizing the Church and community on the need for care and counsel as mission is a major function of Oasis Africa. From many preaching engagements, media interviews, and storytelling, we have exemplified this model especially after several critical incidents: Westgate Mall terror attack (September 2013), the Garissa University College massacre (April 2015), and other occasions. We also ensure that we care for caregivers who include parents, pastors and missionaries, training them on self-care, other care and organizational care especially in stress management, work-life balance, vicarious trauma and compassion fatigue.

Conclusion

This paper has presented the reality that the Church of Jesus Christ is growing fast especially in the global South. This growth represents over-all gain for the global Church. However, there is also a multiplication of social, relational and emotional needs that threaten wholeness of individuals and communities where the Church is mushrooming, especially in Africa. Care and counsel as mission is a sure means of using Church-based resources to meet mental health and trauma needs within the Church. In particular, Africa has her share of these needs given the poverty, conflict and strife within some African nations as well as the outcomes of the AIDS pandemic. However, as much as the Continent bows under this load of care, there are indigenous resources therein that the Church can mobilize to provide for the needs of her members as well as community. This presentation argues that harnessing these resources and training Church members to utilize them is the call of God on the global Church at this time and age. Finally, we propose the Oasis Africa three-legged model as a means of harnessing holistic care and counsel knowledge from truthful psychology models, the Christian discipline and the wealth of African indigenous resources to create care and counsel models that the Church can utilize for the ministry of care and counsel.

References

Akokpari, J.K. (2002). The State, Refugees and Migration in Sub-Saharan Africa. *International Migration*, 36, 211–234.

Beck, Aaron (1996). "The Past and the Future of Cognitive Therapy". *Journal of Psychotherapy Practice and Research*, 6(4), 276–284.

Bouverot, A. (2014). Director General of the GSMA. *http://www.gsma.com/newsroom/press-release/gsma-report-forecasts-half-a-billion-mobile-subscribers-ssa-2020/* [accessed Oct 6, 2016].

CAK (2014). Communication Authority of Kenya. http://www.ca.go.ke/index.php/what-we-do/94-news/285-kenya-s-mobile-penetration-hits-80-per-cent [accessed Oct 6, 2016].

GSMA. (2014). *Mobile economy: 2014.* Retrieved from http://www.gsmamobileeconomy.com/ [accessed Oct 6, 2016].

Jenkins, Philip. (2011). *The Next Christendom: The Coming of Global Christianity*. Oxford University Press, NY.

Keene Reder, E. A. (2006). Grief and Bereavement. In Gwyther, L., Merriman, A., Sebuiya, L.M. & Schietinger H, (eds). *A Clinical Guide to Supportive and Palliative Care for HIV/AIDS*. Alexandra, VA: Global Partners in Care.

Kimenyi, M.S. & Datta, A. (2011). *Think tanks in sub-Saharan Africa. How the political Landscape has influenced their origins.* London, UK: Overseas Development Institute. Retrieved from https://www.odi.org/sites/odi.org.uk/files/odi-assets/publications-opinion-files/7527.pdf [accessed Oct 6, 2016].

Mobie, T. R. (2005). *The Persistent Traumatic Experience of Poverty among Refugees from Mozambique living in the Bushbuckridge Area. A Challenge to Pastoral Care.* Masters Thesis. Pretoria, South Africa: Faculty of Theology, University of Pretoria. January 26, 2015, http://repository.up.ac.za/handle/2263/26612 [accessed Oct 6, 2016].

Mwiti, G. K. & Dueck, A. (2006). *Christian counseling: An African indigenous perspective.* Pasadena, CA: Fuller Seminary Press.

Mwiti, Gladys K. (2005). *Moving On Towards Maturity*. Nairobi, Kenya: Evangel Publishing House.

Ndii, D. (2004). *Role and development of microfinance and savings and credit cooperatives in Africa.* Paper presented at Nairobi Stock Exchange Golden Jubilee and 8th African Stock Exchanges Association (ASEA) Conference 23-26 November, 2004. Nairobi, Kenya. Kenya Leadership Institute.

UNAIDS (2014). *Fact Sheet.* January 24, 2015, *http://www.unaids.org/en/re sources/campaigns/2014/2014gapreport/factsheet* [accessed Oct 6, 2016].

UNICEF. (2014). *The state of the world's children 2014 in numbers: Every child counts.* Retrieved from http://www.unicef.org/sowc2014/numbers/#statistics [accessed Oct 6, 2016].

UNHCR (2015). UNHCR and partners seek US$331 million to help refugees from Central African Republic. UNHCR. Accessed on January 23, 2015. http://www.unhcr.org/54c24f356.html [accessed Oct 6, 2016].

Wilberforce, W. (2006). *Real Christianity.* Ventura, CA: Regal Books.

Promoting Mental Health at Congregational Level

Beate Jakob

1. Introduction

For almost 110 years the German Institute for Medical Mission (DIFAEM)[1] has been engaged in promoting Christian health services worldwide—in partnership with Christian churches and organizations. DIFAEM's work is based on the conviction that Christians, Christian communities and churches have a healing ministry which is an essential part of their mission, and that they can contribute to health in a specific way. The health projects DIFAEM develops and supports reflect a dynamic and holistic concept of health and healing that includes the spiritual and social dimension of health.[2]

In the implementation of health projects together with partners DIFAEM applies the principles of Primary Health Care the World Health Organization (WHO) promoted in 1978.[3] Primary Health Care is a people-centered bottom-up approach to health whereby people at local level are the main actors. Instead of offering interventions in a top-down manner, PHC facilitates participation and gives space for solutions created and owned by communities which use their own strengths. Thus, the former selective and mostly curative approach to health has been broadened by measures that promote health and prevent ill-health. Primary Health Care reflects the knowledge that health and healing are not only and sometimes not primarily medical issues. The improvement of health needs a comprehensive multidimensional approach. In 2008, 30 years after the proclamation of Primary Health Care, the WHO's World Health Report entitled "Primary Health Care Now more than ever" strongly advocated for the revitalization of Primary Health Care.[4]

In 2014, DIFAEM hosted an international symposium on "Christian Responses to Health and Development". The main questions the participants discussed were: "What are the characteristics of Christian health services in

---

[1] www.difaem.de.
[2] Cf. Jakob & Laepple, Gesundheit.
[3] Online: http://www.who.int/topics/primary_health_care/en/
[4] World Health Organization, Primary Health Care.

our time and how can Christian health services become partners of the formal health system?" Among the main characteristics of Christian health services that the participants identified were the inclusion of the spiritual dimension in health care, and the focus on community based approaches to health.

2. What faith communities can contribute to health—the "Religious Health Assets" model

Churches and Christian communities significantly contribute to health, especially in resource limited settings. However, Christian health services are not always aligned with the formal health system. While most governments appreciate Christian health services, only a few are ready to allocate an appropriate share of the national health budget to the health work of the churches. Why?

These are just some of the reasons:

- ➢ Historically, the churches themselves did not actively seek a close cooperation with the formal health system, especially as long as they had enough funds from other, mostly overseas sources.

- ➢ So far, the churches' contribution to health has not been documented properly. Most of their huge health work, especially the work of communities, is literally not "on the map".

- ➢ Sometimes, there has also been a problem of communication between governments and the churches. Representatives of the governments might say that, "These church people are people of good will who do a lot of good. We need them. But nobody knows exactly what they are doing. It's sometimes even difficult to understand them as they use their own faith language."

- ➢ Moreover, faith communities themselves often are not aware of what they actually contribute to health.

How then can we understand and document the contribution of faith communities to health? How can we make this contribution known to the communities themselves as well as the public? How can we bring church health services on the map? These questions led to establishing the "African Religious Health Assets Programme" (ARHAP) in 2001—today: "International Religious Health Assets Programme" (IRHAP)[5]. IRHAP is a collaborative re-

---

[5] http://www.irhap.uct.ac.za/

search network based at the University of Cape Town. Its aim is to document the contribution of religion and of religious communities to health, and to align church based health services with the formal health system.

According to IRHAP, faith communities contribute to health because they own "Religious Health Assets" (RHAs). RHAs are strengths, potentials, resources, in Biblical terms it is the "talents" of faith communities that promote health. Tangible or visible health assets of faith communities like the provision of medical services or groups caring for others are well known and appreciated. In addition, faith communities own so-called intangible, invisible health assets. These are rooted in the spiritual dimension and the motivational and mobilizing capacity of faith communities. These assets like trust, motivation, credibility, compassion, mutual support, honesty, prayer, moral authority, etc. can play an important part in fostering the health of individuals and communities. However, as it is difficult to assess these assets and to measure their impact on health, they are often overlooked.

Within the framework of IRHAP's research programme, a matrix to make the nature of religious health assets understandable was developed. Of course,

Religious Health Assets

		Direct	Indirect
Religious Health Assets	Intangible	❏ Prayer ❏ Resilience ❏ Health-seeking Behaviour ❏ Motivation ❏ Responsibility ❏ Commitment/Sense of Duty ❏ Relationship: Caregiver & "Patient" ❏ Advocacy/Prophetic ❏ Resistance - Physical and/or Structural/Political	❏ Individual (Sense of Meaning) ❏ Belonging - Human/Divine ❏ Access to Power/Energy ❏ Trust/Distrust ❏ Faith - Hope - Love ❏ Sacred Space in a Polluting World (AIC) ❏ Time ❏ Emplotment (Story)
	Tangible	❏ Infrastructure ❏ Hospitals - Beds, etc ❏ Clinics ❏ Dispensaries ❏ Training - Para-Medical ❏ Hospices ❏ Funding/Development Agencies ❏ Holistic Support ❏ Hospital Chaplains ❏ Faith Healers ❏ Traditional Healers ❏ Care Groups ❏ NGO/FBO - "projects"	❏ Manyano and other fellowships ❏ Choir ❏ Education ❏ Sacraments/Rituals ❏ Rites Of Passage (Accompanying) ❏ Funerals ❏ Network/Connections ❏ Leadership Skills ❏ Presence in the "Bundu" (on the margins) ❏ Boundaries (Normative)

Continuum → Health Outcomes

this matrix reflects only a theory, but it is a helpful concept to widen our perception of the health assets owned by faith communities.[6]

This matrix includes four quadrants. Along the vertical axis are the tangible and intangible health assets. Along its horizontal axis the matrix distinguishes between assets with a direct and those with an indirect health outcome.

Talking about the impact on health, one usually refers to the assets in the bottom-left quadrant of the matrix which are the tangible health assets with a direct positive impact on health, e.g. hospitals, care & counseling groups etc. These assets can be measured and quantified. Among the tangible health assets having an indirect impact on health are for instance groups that create relationships, like the choir which can also have a positive impact on health, and rituals. These tangible assets are usually not regarded as health promoting. But they often do have a positive impact on health.

The two upper quadrants refer to intangible religious health assets, graded according to their direct or indirect impact on health—like prayer and resilience which are directly related to health, and a sense of meaning and faith/hope/love which are assets not directly linked to health, but with a major impact on health. These assets are much more difficult to assess than the tangible ones as they are not quantifiable but have to be assessed through qualitative methods.

In terms of mental health, it is especially these intangible religious health assets that are important. The RHA matrix was initially designed to demonstrate and document the contribution of faith communities to health with regard to HIV&AIDS. For people affected by HIV&AIDS it is obviously very important to have access to treatment and care. But we also know that belonging to a social network as well as having hope and trust affects these patients' physical and even more their mental health significantly.

The concept of Religious Health Assets helps to make the comprehensive contribution of faith communities to health understandable. Health promotion at community level goes beyond providing tangible health services and also goes beyond counseling and praying for the sick. Moreover, this concept demonstrates that the genuine contribution of faith communities to health is not a special task, an add-on to what is being done already. The majority of these religious health assets, especially the intangible ones, are an integral part of everyday life of the community. The community as a social network and a place of worship is a healing place in itself.

---

[6] Cochrane, Religious Health Assets, 24.

3. Integration of mental health in community based approaches—a brief overview on DIFAEM's projects in countries of the global South

So far, mental health is not really included in community based approaches in the so-called low-income countries. The graph shows the rate of outpatient mental health facilities per 100.000 people with regard to the World Bank Income Groups.[7]

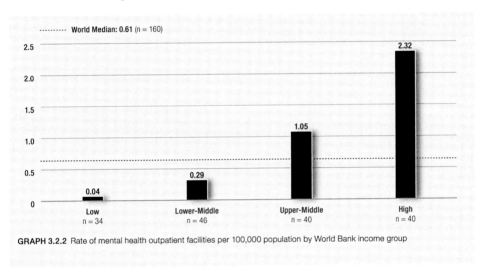

GRAPH 3.2.2 Rate of mental health outpatient facilities per 100,000 population by World Bank income group

DIFAEM, too, did not focus on mental health in its Primary Health Care projects over the past decades. There is plenty of experience with community based approaches in projects primarily addressing physical health issues like HIV&AIDS, malaria, tuberculosis and Ebola as well as mother and child health. But actually most of the community based projects have included a mental health component from the beginning, or mental health issues emerged during project implementation.—The WHO was right when they coined the sentence: "No health without mental health".[8]

To give some examples:

In the **Democratic Republic of the Congo** DIFAEM runs projects for traumatized women. These women need medical treatment like restorative surgeries, financial support and they surely benefit from trainings and edu-

---

[7] Source: WHO Mental Health Atlas 2011. Online accessible: http://www.who.int/mental_health/publications/mental_health_atlas_2011/en/
[8] Cf. WHO, Fact sheet: http://www.who.int/mediacentre/factsheets/fs220/en/

cation. But to be healed they need a healing community that takes them up and helps them to gradually regain hope, trust and dignity.

In the **Ebola work in West Africa** during the acute phase of the epidemic the focus was on bringing the epidemic to a halt by providing protection materials and by training health workers and people in the communities. But after this first phase it appeared that "Ebola survivors" and many health workers are severely traumatized. According to estimates of church partners in Liberia and Sierra Leone up to 60 percent of Ebola survivors suffer from post-traumatic stress disorder. For them, too, the community will be of help through the above mentioned intangible direct and indirect health assets.

In **Raxaul, India**, a town close to the border to Nepal, DIFAEM has been supporting a community based HIV&AIDS project of a Christian hospital since 2010. Last year the project team came up with a project proposal towards integrating mental health in the community based project. They had realized that there is a high and growing rate of depression and suicide in the catchment area of the hospital, partly caused by gender based violence.

In a project in **Malawi** it just recently turned out that mental health is one of the issues that can't be neglected in communities and at the same time can be addressed by them. Since 2011, DIFAEM has been implementing a project that strictly applies the principles of Primary Health Care. In the communities of the catchment area of a Presbyterian and a Catholic health centre, people at local level are engaged in a process of improving the health of their communities. At the beginning of this project the communities performed a community and asset mapping and learnt about the religious health assets.

Asked about "What contributes to health in your community?" people mentioned mainly the following factors: The services of the health centre, safe water sources, nutrition, availability of drugs. But, their list also comprised some of the intangible factors like mutual respect, relationships, and prayer.

In another exercise the people listed their health concerns. They mentioned malnutrition, lack of safe water, cultural practices with a negative impact on health, drinking locally brewed beer etc. Thereafter they were asked to bear in mind their health assets and to think about who has the capacity and who is responsible to tackle their health concerns: The community, the health centre, or the government? The result was quite encouraging showing that the communities attributed almost all health concerns to their own capacity and responsibility.

Most of the health concerns can be addressed by the community itself.

As a next step, the communities ranked their health concerns and developed respective action plans. All participating communities ranked sanitation and nutrition on top. They focused on tangible things to be tackled by using assets like manpower and materials. But alongside building pit latrines, hand washing facilities, digging rubbish pits a.s.o., they continued discussing health issues and health assets. For a long time mental health issues were not mentioned at all. It took three years for people to come up with sensitive issues like alcoholism, gender based violence, teenage pregnancies, prostitution, depression, and the issue of suicide. These taboo issues are now being addressed after the communities have been walking a long way together. Currently, these issues are discussed in community meetings before the church elders and the traditional authorities. People ask how to use their own assets to tackle these issues. Issues of gender based violence and alcohol abuse definitely cannot be improved by imposed strategies or through legislation. These issues are related to cultural norms and behaviour patterns that can only be changed in a very slow process of transformation. In this process intangible religious health assets like mutual trust and good relationships are essential. There are now plans to train the community health workers in mental health issues so that they can detect mental disorders and offer basic counseling services.

4. Congregations promote mental health—a pilot project in Germany

A project on "Congregations and Depression" is being performed by DIFAEM and the Department of Practical Theology at the Theological Faculty of Tübingen in cooperation with health professionals forming an "Alliance against Depression" ("Bündnis gegen Depression"). Funds are provided by the "Stiftung Diakonie Württemberg".

1. Why does DIFAEM run such a project in German congregations and why on depression?

DIFAEM aims at improving access to quality health care for people in resource limited settings. Why then does DIFAEM run a project in a church in Germany where most people still have access to a very high standard of health care?

> ➤ First, European communities in general and congregations in particular should rediscover their role in health and become active partners of the formal health sector.

> ➤ Second, there is a window of opportunity to introduce experiences of DIFAEM's work with communities of the Global South in Germany where many people are disappointed by a purely biomedical approach to health. In their search for health and wholeness people are open to approaches including the social and spiritual dimension of healing.

Why a project on depression? It was decided to tackle depression not only because the number of people suffering from depression is increasing constantly, but also because depression is a disease that affects the person as a whole. Of course, this is true for each disease. Even a broken leg has implications beyond the physical dimension. But it is especially true for depression. It deeply affects the person's relationship to him- or herself, to fellow human beings and also and often particularly to God.

The research questions of the project on "Congregations and Depression" was defined as, "How can congregations in their capacity as social networks and places of worship assist people suffering from depression?"

The definition of 'depression' used in the project does not end with the diagnostic classification system but takes into account a wider phenomenal domain. However, in dealing with this topic people are made aware that there is a difference between 'depression' in the sense of an illness which severely affects people for a longer period on the one side, and the condition of being in a depressed mood which everybody experiences from time to time.

2. The project design

The project has been implemented in four stages:

- Online questionnaire
- 25 qualitative semi-structured interviews
- Development of resource materials for congregations
- Implementation in three congregations

3. Research-findings

3.1 Online questionnaire

An online questionnaire was sent to all pastors serving in a church district. The response rate was 32%. In 16,3 % of all pastoral counseling sessions the consulters are people suffering from depressions. The majority of the pastors (62%) don't feel well prepared for counseling depressive persons. More than 90% of depressive people are concerned about religious topics like guilt, feeling God to be absent and wondering about a God who allows them to suffer.

3.2 Qualitative data

The interviewees were selected through purposive sampling. They represented the groups of persons affected and their relatives, health experts like psychologists in counseling centres, ministers, and volunteers.

Here are some of the results of the semi structured interviews.

The main questions of the interviews conducted with depressive persons and their relatives concerned their experiences with congregations and their expectations with regard to congregations.

- **Persons affected by depression**: As a common feature they long for relationships with others but at the same time feel unable or "not worthy" to be related to others. They feel stigmatized as the disease is still a taboo in church and society. While for some of them the congregation is a place where they feel welcome, the majority is not integrated in a congregation.

A man suffering from depression still remembers well the sermons held by the pastor of the congregation he was a member of when he was young. At the time his mother suffered from depression, in his sermons this pastor frequently talked about mental disorder to be caused by personal sin. Up to today the man feels deeply affected and hurt by the message the pastor was giving about mental diseases.

In spite of negative experiences with congregations, some people say that their personal faith helps them to cope with their disease. In particular very short prayers or Bible verses are of help to them.

What they expect from the congregation is: First and foremost they wish the congregation to be better informed about the disease. People should know that it is not a lack of will power to get up in the morning but a matter of not being able to do so. And the same applies to the fact that people suffering from depression are definitely not able to work on a regular basis. Depression should not be regarded as being rooted in personal failure but has to be recognized and accepted as a disease like any other.

Here are some specific suggestions: People suffering from depression wish to be included in the congregation by doing some kind of voluntary work. Such work should not ask too much from them, but just give them the chance to feel respected and to do something useful like one interviewee who was happy to serve at parish meals from time to time. Some people would appreciate liturgical services to leave more space for silence and meditation.

> **Relatives:** Many relatives, especially parents, consider themselves guilty of the family member's sickness, especially at the beginning. They feel helpless and unable to cope with the situation of living with a relative being severely ill, whom they feel to be "far away" from them, and whom they can't really help. For most of them the congregation hasn't been of help. They feel what a parish offers doesn't really relate to their lives. According to their experience the parish members don't have an eye for them like one of them puts it: "No one of the congregation approached me and asked if I needed help."

Among their requests they mention the need for working against misconceptions by sensitizing and providing information about depression in congregations. They would welcome to be assisted by visits and practical help. Moreover, they would appreciate talking to the pastor and joining meditation exercises.

- **Volunteers:** Just to give one positive example, the leader of a church choir offers participation to people affected by mental disorders. The choir's first aim is not achievement but it serves as a strong social network. According to the choir leader it is most important that choir members feel welcome no matter what their condition is. She says: "Everybody can just be the way he or she is." The choir members treat each other with care. They call or visit each other in times of distress thus forming a social network. At the same time the spiritual dimension of the song repertoire is important. According to the choir leader, "Singing spiritual songs like hymns of praise sometimes makes people cry" what she encourages explicitly. This choir is an example of an intangible religious health asset.

- **Pastors:** The interviews with the pastors focused on their counseling services. Pastors often feel helpless when dealing with people affected by depression. Not being able to help people by talking to and praying with them is, as one of them put it, "like driving in total darkness". Pastors complain about lack of skills in how to interact with depressive people, especially in terms of knowing when it is necessary to draw clear boundaries e.g. if congregation members want to consult them almost daily. Questions of sin, guilt and personal failure are frequent issues in pastoral counseling. Sometimes it is difficult to discern between real guilt and inadequate feelings of being guilty as part of the disease pattern. Therefore, pastors strongly request more information about depression to be available and advise strongly these questions to become part of the education and formation of future pastors.

Looking at the quantitative and qualitative data ways of how congregations can deal with depression were identified. Important are/is:

- Information about the disease pattern and thus taking depression out of the taboo zone and into the congregation.

- Inclusion of sick persons in day-to-day parish activities or inviting them to participate in church groups are of great importance.

- Theological discussions on misconceptions in terms of guilt and personal failure relating to the causes and course of depression.

- Further trainings for pastors and volunteers.

4. Developing resource materials for congregations and first implementation phase

The project team together with the health professionals of the "Association against Depression" designed a bunch of activities which were tested in two congregations and thereafter adapted and published.

This resource book includes:

> - Information on medical aspects of depression and on spirituality and depression.
> - Chapters on conversation skills and pastoral counseling.
> - A template of a thematic Sunday service including a sermon on theological aspects of depression.
> - A Bible study on depression tackling questions of, "Does faith help to prevent depression? Is there a link between depression and guilt?"
> - Confirmation classes that focus on questions like, "What builds me up—what drags me down?"[9]

5. Implementation in three congregations

In the implementation phase a participatory approach was applied with three congregations.

The congregations formed a project group that was briefed about the background of the project and got some basic information about the nature of depression. For a second meeting the project group invited representatives of the congregations and the church, health professionals of the diaconic services, general practitioners and pharmacists, and representatives of the civil society.

With this group a mapping exercise was done. The participants created a map of the congregation and of secular groups/organizations within the congregation by identifying groups, important persons, meeting points that might play a role in tackling mental health issues and noting them on cards. Different colors were chosen for church groups and the secular entities. In

---

[9] Weyel & Jakob, Menschen.

addition, relationships between the various groups were marked by connecting the respective cards with lines.

The map they came up with showed the assets of the congregation with their links to other church or secular assets. Within the congregation they mapped, for example, women's groups, communication teams, grief groups, a pastoral counseling team etc. Among the secular entities that were put on the map were the general practitioner, the pharmacy, groups visiting terminally ill persons etc. The lines marking the linkages between the assets showed that a good number of church groups are not well cross-linked.

This exercise was an eye-opener both to the congregation members and the representatives of the formal health system. Even the congregation members didn't know all the church activities and groups. Referring to a counseling group in the congregation a general practitioner said: "For some of my patients it is equally important to receive a contact address as to get a prescription. Now I know where to connect them." A pharmacist said: "So far, I have been aware of only about 20 percent of the groups existing here."

Already this first step of the project implementation was an important outcome: The congregations entered into a process of networking and establishing links to the formal health sector.

In one of the congregations the respective meeting was attended by the promoter of an initiative of the civil community named "Healthy Community Eningen" (Eningen is a community in South Germany). Here, important links to the civil society could be established during the very first meeting of the project group.

Following this first meeting, the project groups were asked to meet without the project coordinator and to set up an individual implementation plan. The leading question was, "How can we meet the expectations of people with depression and their relatives within our congregation and by using our particular assets?"

The three participating congregations developed individual implementation plans each having a slightly different focus. One of the congregations chose the motto of "How can we promote healing accompaniment in our congregation?" Another one focused on the issue of "depression and personal guilt". From the beginning of the project people started to talk about depression and about how they could include persons of whom they knew that they suffered from depression again and again. People said: "We have to be aware of who is missing in our services or in group meetings. Let's follow them up instead of just leaving them aside because we feel unable to meet the expectations of a person who is deeply depressed."

Here are the main activities that were conducted:

- All participating congregations celebrated thematic Sunday services. The Sunday service serves as an important platform to create awareness about the frequency of mental disorders so that people become aware that "Christians get depression, too".
- Psychiatrists and psychotherapists provided information about the character of mental disorders.
- In one congregation the two pastors started open counseling hours once a week and offer people to be personally blessed after the Sunday service.
- Volunteers like group leaders and the members of an already existing counseling group got further trainings that instructed them about the nature of depression and mental disorders and taught them some conversation techniques and pastoral counseling approaches.
- Confirmation classes about mobbing and depression were held.
- Bible studies were performed on "depression and guilt".
- After events or lectures "safe spaces" were offered to share personal issues in small groups.

In these congregations issues of mental health were prominent over a period of appr. six months.

These are the main experiences the congregations share in reflective meetings:

- As there are still a lot of misconceptions in congregations concerning mental disorders, it proved to be essential to create awareness about mental disorders in general and depression in particular and to provide sound information about the disease, its various causes, its impact on people's lives, and the available therapies.
- The pastors are very surprised that instead of only learning and talking about depression, it has been possible to reach people suffering from depression and their relatives. Many people were ready to talk about themselves. All pastors mentioned that depression has become a major issue in their pastoral counseling.
- People very much appreciated the "safe spaces" to share their experiences.

- Even people who are more distant to the congregation visited the project events.

- Congregation members mentioned that "It is good to openly address issues around depression. It was a taboo in spite of all of us knowing depression being a major problem within the congregation."

- Representatives of the local "Alliance against Depression" are very impressed by congregations taking up the issue and regard the project as the starting point of a fruitful cooperation. Thus, congregations have entered into a process of being linked to the formal health sector.

- The local newspapers and some church related radio stations reported about the project.

- A 40-year old women suffering from depression very much appreciated that the project hasn't just promoted praying for people suffering from depression but focused on sensitizing and informing. Therefore, she dared to openly talk about her experiences and that she had felt to be stigmatized within the congregation.

The congregations are planning to continue after the current project phase. For example, there are plans to offer a safe space for people seeking advice and counseling once a month after the Sunday service. This might result in a process of transformation whereby people with depression or other mental health disorders and their relatives feel at home in a congregation that offers a safe space for them.

5. One of my personal experiences

Let me add a personal experience which is related to the man. In my home congregation we offer a "space for listening". This is a kind of safe space where a group of volunteers provide an "open ear" for people with various needs. People can make an appointment by e-mail or by leaving a message on an answering machine. One of the persons I listened to is a 45 year-old man who holds a high position within a business organization. As we met for the first time he was deeply depressive and saw no way out. "Sometimes I wish my life was just over", he said. Only when he told me that he was in psychiatric therapy and had an appointment on the same day, I offered to enter into a process of listening and talking and agreed to meet again the following week. After our initially weekly sessions we have kept meeting in longer intervals up to this day. When we talk to each other, we focus on his resources/assets, especially the social and the spiritual ones that help him to cope with situations of insecurity and distress, and we think about how he might further develop his resources. For me, it was amazing to see that after some time life came back to this man who had been totally without hope and without any prospect for his future. He claims that for him this "open ear" has been like crutches in times he felt unable to move forward by his own means.

What we do in this "space of listening" is just being present for people in need and to actively listen to them. Sometimes this helps people to find their own solutions, sometimes we are complementary to the professional therapy, and sometimes we convince people to consult the health professionals. In our congregation promotion of mental health started with this initiative. In the course of time we added special services for people in need and, most important: There is a growing general awareness of persons with mental disorders in our congregation.

6. Lessons learnt

Over the past years I learnt that:

> ➤ Faith communities own assets to promote mental health especially through their intangible health assets.

> ➤ In some of DIFAEM's community based projects in the global South mental health issues have either been included already or are emerging and can be addressed in local communities.

> ➤ In Germany (we might also say: in Europe) there is a window of opportunity to mobilize congregations to address mental health issues. Congregations can and should become partners of the formal health system.

References

Cochrane, J. (2006). Religious Health Assets (RHAs)—Conceptual and Theoretical Framework. In: Deutsches Institut für Ärztliche Mission (Ed.), *Religion, faith and public health. Documentation on a consultation; 9–11 February 2006* (pp. 14–45). Tübingen: DIFAEM.

Jakob, B., & Laepple, U. (2014). *Gesundheit, Heilung und Spiritualität. Heilende Dienste in Kirche, Diakonie und weltweiter Ökumene.* Neukirchen-Vluyn: Neukirchener Theologie.

Jakob, B., & Weyel, B. (2014). *Menschen mit Depression. Orientierungen und Impulse für die Praxis in Kirchengemeinden*. Gütersloh: Gütersloher Verlagshaus.

Materials on PHC including the Alma Ata Proclamation of PHC. Retrieved from http://www.who.int/topics/primary_health_care/en/ [accessed July 10, 2015].

Mental health: Strengthening our Response—WHO Fact sheet N°220, Updated August 2014. Retrieved from http://www.who.int/mediacentre/factsheets/fs220/en/ [accessed July 10, 2015].

WHO Mental Health Atlas 2011. Retrieved from http://www.who.int/mental_health/publications/mental_health_atlas_2011/en/ [accessed July 10, 2015].

World Health Organization, & Lerberghe, W. v. (2008). *The World Health Report 2008. Primary Health Care. Now more than ever*. Geneva, Switzerland: World Health Organization.

Equipping the Church as a Caring Community

Samuel Pfeifer

This article has grown out of my background as the medical director of a Christian psychiatric clinic in Switzerland—Clinic Sonnenhalde near Basel (www.sonnenhalde.ch).[1] For over 25 years, I had the privilege to serve our patients, but also to reflect our calling as Christian professionals in today's health challenges. Moreover, I had the opportunity to visit psychiatric clinics around the globe, from China to Senegal. Over five years, our clinic had a partnership with a secular clinic in Bulgaria. The director had asked us to help them reform their hospital and to apply the lessons we had learned in our clinic. I still remember our first visit in this institution, way out of the city, a few concrete buildings in a village, the stench of urine in the stairways, the locked doors, and the patients crammed in small rooms without any recreational space or any activity. We were in a foreign land, and did not speak the language—but we felt the crying need of the patients and we also sensed the honest desire of Dr. Genova to change this place. Over the years, we witnessed a fascinating change, which resulted in a truly humane and caring institution for those suffering patients, who are being locked away in so many societies of the world.

"There is no health without mental health"[2] – what a bold statement in a world, where mental illness is still shamefully hidden, rejected and demonized! What a bold statement in countries like India or China, which have the highest rate of suicides in the world! What a bold statement in provinces, where there is no other treatment for severe mental illness than locking them up in jail![3] Famous anthropologist Arthur Kleinman is decrying the failure in humanity regarding mental health.[4]

However, there is hope: It is very encouraging that Christians are starting to focus on the desperate need of those who are afflicted with mental distress, sorrow and illness. This article is intended to give an overview

---

[1] An earlier version of this article has appeared 2014 in the Doon Theological Journal (India), 11(2), 144–155.
[2] Prince et al., No Health, 859–877.
[3] Sharma, Mental Health, 495.
[4] Kleinman, Global Mental Health, 603–604.

of Biblical perspectives related to mental health and originated in a presentation given at the first conference on "A Christian view of Mental Health" which was held at the Luther New Theological Seminary in Dehradun / India in 2013.

To be honest, in India, the need has been seen already many years ago. One of the major beacons of hope was the foundation of the Nur Manzil hospital in Lucknow UP.[5] Nur Manzil Psychiatric Centre was established in 1950 by Dr. E. Stanley Jones (1884–1973), a renowned American Methodist Missionary, evangelist, ecumenical leader, statesman, author, a dynamic personality and a friend of India since 1907. The founder firmly believed in the psychological and spiritual healing and wellbeing of mentally afflicted. Moreover, the Vellore Christian Medical College has had a psychiatry department for many years, training medical doctors and psychologists in the field of mental health. Certainly, there are many more initiatives I am not aware of. Nonetheless, it seems that the professional care for a few suffering patients in privileged places is now spreading to the churches of the world who are increasingly becoming aware of the needs of mentally burdened individuals and their families, binding up the broken-hearted.

What is the basis of this new emphasis in Christian ministry in the Global Mental Health movement? When the prophets of the Old Testament announced the coming Messiah, they pointed out several levels of his ministry: (a) a redirection of the people's hearts towards God (Ez. 36:26ff); (b) a political calling to free the captives and the oppressed (Isa. 42:7); and (c) a healing ministry, opening the eyes of the blind (Isa. 42:7) and healing the wounded (Isa. 30:26). The church, over the centuries, has continued to carry out this calling all over the world. Regarding medical missions, the church has brought medical help to the remotest areas of the world, and is still a primary source in providing health care for the marginalized and the poor.

However, as a psychiatrist, I read one more role of the Messiah's ministry and thus the church's ministry: "binding up the brokenhearted and comforting all who mourn." (Isa. 61:1ff.; Jer. 31:13). Although the emphasis on "mental health" in a Christian context seems to be relatively new, there has been a longstanding tradition of integration in other countries. Whereas the term "psyche" is already to be found in the New Testament (translated as "soul" or "heart"), systematic research in the field of psychology has only started about 150 years ago. In medicine, the specialty of "psychiatry" (dealing with the medical causes and therapies of mental disorders) has long been a rather neglected science. Moreover, the ever evolving field of psycho-

---

[5] www.nurmanzil.org

therapy has caused quite some resistance, but nonetheless became more and more successful.

Traditionally, it had been the church that offered counseling, guidance and support in difficult times. In addition, it was the church, which started to build retreat homes for the depressed as an alternative to inhuman treatments in state mental institutions. Writing before the broad acceptance of modern secular psychology, Old Testament scholar and church historian, Franz Delitzsch (1861), noted that "Biblical psychology is no science of yesterday. It is one of the oldest sciences of the church."[6]

However, the growing influence of psychology, psychotherapy and psychiatry also brought a secularization of the Christian effort to provide soul care. As Eric L. Johnson (2007) in his monumental work "Foundations for Soul Care. A Christian Psychology Proposal,"[7] pointed out, the Christian church has vastly succumbed to scientific modernism, sometimes retaining theological core terms, but actually changing their content. Eventually, "psychology came to be seen by many of its participants, and increasingly by the culture at large, as providing an authoritative replacement for the pronouncements of the Bible, the pope, and church tradition. As a result, by the middle of the twentieth century, secular psychology and psychotherapy was firmly entrenched as the only legitimate approach to the study of human nature and to soul care. Rightly interpreted, modern soul care should be seen as the chief religious competitor to Christian salvation in the West."[8]

Secularism for many decades was the hallmark of scientific psychotherapy and psychiatry. Researchers only observed religiousness in the context of pathology, such as religious delusions or religiously motivated fears. Indeed, such phenomena can occur. However scientific psychiatry for a long time closed its eyes from the fact, that a personal faith in a loving God also can be a resource. It was the research in resilience and into positive psychology[9] which began to bring about a change. Now textbooks were allowed to ask the question "Is Faith Delusion? Why religion is good for your health.[10] Most prolific was the research by Prof. Dr. Harold Koenig at Duke University in the United States, who was able to demonstrate that positive aspects of

---

6 Delitzsch, Psychology, 3.
7 Johnson, Foundations.
8 Johnson, Foundations, 69; see also Vitz, Psychology.
9 Antonowsky, Health.
10 Sims, Faith.

faith by far outweighed negative effects. His findings are regularly being published in some of the leading journals of the field.[11]

Fortunately, there have been new efforts to rethink soul care not only from a humanistic point of view but also in the context of Scripture-based Christian teaching.[12] Several Christian universities in the United States started special programs for the integration of psychology and theology, fulfilling the requirements of the top accrediting boards of the American Psychological Association as well as using Biblical studies to better understand the human nature (e.g. Fuller Theological Seminary, Rosemead School of Psychology or Wheaton College). However, the goal is not just to change the underlying philosophy of soul care, but the challenge is to see the practical needs of suffering people in and around the church.

Statistics of the World Health Organization[13] show an increasing burden of global health with major depression, expressed in the term of DALY = disability-adjusted life years, not only in affluent countries but also in low and middle income societies. Depression does not stop outside the Christian community either. As the Psalms show, even strong believers can be afflicted with low mood, physical weakness and hopelessness. Thus the church is increasingly forced to rethink its strategies in providing mental health and soul care. Moreover, the church should be challenged, not only to look at mental distress and suffering from a Western perspective of relative material security. The church may have unique resources in mental health, even in countries where the services for the mentally suffering are not yet developed in a sufficient way.[14]

Seven Principles

I would like to propose seven principles of mental health care in a Christian context. Mental Health in the church should reflect the following values:

1. Compassion
2. Professionalism and Advocacy
3. Change-Orientation (Admonishing)
4. Comfort and Encouragement
5. Supporting the Weak
6. Patience
7. Hope

---

[11] For example: Bonelli & Koenig, Disorders, 657–673.
[12] Benner, Care.
[13] Funk et al., Mental health.
[14] Raja et al., Evaluating; Patel et al., Efficacy, 33–39.

1. Compassion

When Jesus walked among the crowds, we read that he was "inwardly moved" or "moved with compassion", when he saw them. It is this attitude which we have to learn and to practice again and again. I am aware that in a world with so much poverty and so many socially disadvantaged people, it is not always easy to find the right focus for compassion. Nonetheless, when we really want to reach the mentally suffering, we have to be moved by their distress and the plight of their families.

Compassion was a driving force for the Quakers to build York retreat in Britain, as a bold signal against "lunatic asylums".[15] It was compassion that drove Mennonites in the United States to establish Christian clinics as an alternative to State Mental Hospitals.[16] And I am sure, it was compassion that led to the establishment of Nur Manzil Hospital in Lucknow. Often this attitude of compassion arises from individual confrontation with the terrible destructive power of mental disorder in the life of a person. When a lovely wife and mother of children is suddenly withdrawing, unable to relate anymore, uttering unreasonable self-reproach and even attempting to take her life, then a loving husband may be moved with compassion. But it takes even more effort in compassion to see the members of a church who are suffering, and to take action to improve their plight. Such a compassionate attitude has to be given by the Spirit, and has to be preached and transmitted into social and humanitarian action. Modern psychotherapy even has brought forth a new therapy called "compassion focused therapy"[17] which makes this aspect central for any real change.

2. Professionalism / Advocacy

As the churches are awakening, and regaining their original vision of caring for the "broken-hearted", they are finding themselves in a changed context of medical science and a bio-psycho-social understanding of mental illness. Schizophrenia, depression, epilepsy, dementia, alcohol dependence and other mental, neurological and substance-use (MNS) disorders constitute 13% of the global burden of disease, surpassing both cardiovascular disease and cancer. Prayer and spiritual concerns alone are not enough. Even Jesus, after healing a leprous man, sent him to show himself to the priest (Luke 5:14), the priests being the experts of their times. For the building of the temple Solomon was looking for the best artists. He was looking for professionals.

---

[15] www.theretreatyork.org.uk
[16] Neufeld, Mental Health, 18-31.
[17] Gilbert, Compassion.

Thus, when Christians try to help the underprivileged, benevolence alone is not sufficient. Rather, they will need professional knowledge of the issues, and knowledge of the language of psychology. Psychology has become a major "lingua franca" (a universal language) in our postmodern times. Christian professionals have to understand and to speak this language, however, without adopting all the values which are sometimes attached to psychological views of the human condition. An excellent example for such bridge building between science and the church is the book "Spirituality and Psychiatry" by three British psychiatrists.[18]

In my comparative studies between clinical psychiatry and Biblical teaching,[19] I found that the basic model of biological, social and psychological elements in mental disorders, which have been conceptualized in medical psychiatry, can be found in the Bible as well. As a medical doctor who loves structured texts, I sometimes suffer from the fact that the Bible is not a textbook. However, reading scriptures with open eyes, we can find the same lines which are being drawn in today's psychiatry. Even the use of remedies can be found in the Bible. Prophets used them, even Jesus occasionally employed remedies. Modern medications are much more sophisticated, but they can be regarded as integral part of wholesome treatment of mental disorders.

The next four values of Christian mental health care are taken from just one single verse in the first letter to the Thessalonians, where Paul is concisely summing up elements of effective soul care (1. Thessalonians 5:14). The text not only shows four strategies but also differentiates various states of mind which require different approaches:

Admonishing	–	the idle and disruptive
Encouragement	–	the disheartened, the anxious
Supporting	–	the weak
Patience	–	all

In the language of medicine we would talk of differential indications and differential therapeutic strategies. These may seem very simplistic at first sight, but in my discussions with theologically oriented Christian counselors I sometimes encountered attitudes such as: "If only a person wants to change his or her thinking, the problems will go away!" Or "If only a person trusts his or her life to the Lord, and completely gives his or her life to Jesus, then the mental suffering will be changed into joy!" or "If only a person admits his

---

[18] Cook et al., Spirituality.
[19] Pfeifer, Supporting.

or her sins, and is delivered from demonic bondage, then freedom will follow!" Let us therefore have a look at the differential therapeutic strategies:

3. Change Orientation / Admonishing

Behavioral change and the change of thinking patterns (cognitive change) indeed often are necessary to improve the condition of a person. The term here is translated with words like: admonish, guide, correct, adjust, pull up. However, what are the targeted problems? The persons, who need admonishing, are described as "idle, disordered or unruly". We could also describe them as the socially deviant with adjustment disorders, with antisocial behavior, addiction problems or with self-harming behaviors. Indeed a high percentage of mental problems are associated with addictive disorders and dysfunctional behavior. Cognitive behavioral therapy is the treatment of choice to address these disorders.

The professional counselor has to differentiate which behavior is associated with such "disordered" behavior, and which is associated with social withdrawal, self-neglect or disorganized behavior commonly found in severe mental disorders such as schizophrenia.

4. Encouragement / Comfort

The second group which the apostle Paul identifies is the discouraged, the anxious or the disheartened, as the term is rendered in various translations. In modern terms, one could also talk of those with low self-esteem, depression or anxious-dependent personality disorder or of those who are mourning over the loss of a loved one.

Just telling them to change their thinking is not sufficient. The desire for rest and comfort is a basic human need addressed already by the prophets and later by Jesus. God is described as a "God of comfort". Empathic listening, loving encouragement and soothing words of comfort often help more than "biblical admonition" or doubting their relationship with God. And those loving words are not less Biblical than admonition! They lay a foundation for the usually long way of recovery from depression or grief, bringing out the deep values of the power of faith and fellowship in the hard times of life.

5. Supporting the Weak

When I first noticed this third group of therapeutic indications, I had to pause and ponder the term of the "weak". Who are they that they are honored with a separate strategy of counseling? A preliminary definition of the weak could be "those, who despite their willingness and their desires seem to be unable to adapt to the requirements of a functional life."

Weakness also has a connotation of incurability in a medical sense. Paul describes the thorn in his flesh, so painful that he described it as a messenger of Satan tormenting him. When Paul earnestly cried to God to relieve his attacks of severe pain, he did not experience healing. Rather he was told: "My grace is sufficient for you, for my power is made perfect in weakness." And he concludes: "Therefore I will boast all the more gladly of my weaknesses, so that the power of Christ may rest upon me." (2. Cor 12:9). Weakness seems to be part of the human condition. Thus, Jesus, the high priest, is said to be so afflicted with human suffering and temptation, that he is able to "empathize with our weaknesses" (Hebr. 4:15).

In the field of mental health, we find highly dysfunctional behavior in people with mental retardation or in patients with schizophrenia. Their brain has undergone either organic damage or neuro-biological changes which affect basic behaviors such as caring for themselves, normal eating patterns, social interaction, pursuing their studies or working in a job. Even when they seem stable, they are suffering from a so-called "vulnerability": small amounts of stress can get them out of balance, feeling weak, unable to function in their work or their family environment.

The text tells us not to exhort them, but "to support" them. Medication may alleviate some of their deficiencies, but often they remain in a state of immaturity and dependence, which require the family to provide for them in the most basic forms, even as adults. Often the burden is too heavy for the aging parents. Some of the severely mentally ill run away and end up as homeless people.

What can the church do for them? What could supporting mean in these conditions? In many countries there are programs for the chronically ill, providing sheltered housing plus sheltered employment, teaching them simple ways to support themselves. For example, individuals with mental illness in Uganda, India, the United Republic of Tanzania, Sri Lanka and Ghana who received treatment and support were able to engage in small farming, producing crops and tending poultry, and contributing to their families' food supply.[20] In India there are increasing efforts to bring a mental health perspective to community medicine.[21] And it is encouraging that there seems to be legislation for the cost-free provision of medication in chronic illness such as bipolar or schizophrenic disorder (at least in some states of India, if prescribed in a State mental hospital).

Combining various approaches

Obviously, many patients with mental disorders and distress do not always fit just one category. Thus, a man who has lost his son in a road accident may resort to alcohol to soothe his grief. He might need both consolation in his sorrow, but also admonition in his self-destructive habit of drinking. Or imagine a person with epilepsy who is responding well to medication: she might need support in her illness-related weakness but also admonition to regularly take her medication. And she certainly needs comfort in the grief over her limitations, or the inability to find a husband.

6. Patience

The few examples make it clear that caring for mentally suffering people is no quick fix, not a once for always prayer or action. Rather caring for suffering souls requires a long term perspective. God is a god of patience and long-suffering—and the church is also called to patience in soul care. Endurance requires strength—enduring the fact, that behavioral change often takes time, the recovery from depression may be a long walk through the valley of shadows, and the residual state of schizophrenia will always require some form of support and comfort.

7. Hope

The final requirement for Christian soul care and mental health is hope.

"Is there still hope?" How often doctors are bombarded with this question by patients and relatives alike! Frequently, before I answer, I myself first pose a counter question: "What does 'hope' mean for you?" Do you mean hope of a cure through psychiatry? Hope of healing through God's intervention, or just hope of some improvement in the condition?

---

[20] Astbury & Tebboth, Mental Health.
[21] Srinivasa et al., Schizophrenia, 341–351.

Often patients and their relatives on the one hand, and doctors on the other, are not speaking the same language. As a result people talk too often of a "hopeless case", simply because it does not fit the category of hope for complete restoration. But there are no hopeless cases with God. Faith cannot always provide complete mental health, but it can provide strength and comfort in the midst of weakness, fear, and feelings of rejection.

The Bible points to a hope that reaches beyond the helplessness of our earthly existence to give a person the courage to bear the simply unbearable. At the very point where doctor and pastoral counsellor, medical staff and lay helpers alike run against the barrier of external things that cannot be changed ... at that point, in God's eyes fresh doors open.

I am often asked: What hope can you offer your patients as a psychiatrist and as a Christian? I would like to group my answer into two main areas, namely the medical human perspective (1 to 5) and the biblical point of view (6 to 10).

1. I have hope for individuals with psychiatric problems and illnesses, because experience shows that most disorders improve after a certain time.

2. I have hope, because today, in comparison with earlier times, the suffering involved in psychiatric illness can be moderated or even healed through the help of medication in many more situations than was previously the case.

3. I have hope, because psychiatric problems often provide the opportunity for a new beginning. A crisis in a person's life may be needed, in order to recognize the fragile basis of one's existence and to build one's life on new, firm foundations.

4. I have hope, because I have experienced in many cases that individuals can live a fulfilled life, even with a psychiatric weakness. This applies even with individuals who have pronounced changes of their personality. Even if they have to undergo very difficult experiences, they eventually find their way to a new life within their limitations, after the passage of time.

5. I have hope, because initiatives are increasingly taking place today to provide residential homes and work opportunities for individual suffering from psychiatric illness, in order to ease their lot and support them in shaping their lives. In this connection advocacy groups also bring hope for those who are afflicted and for their families. However, my hope goes beyond these medical and human considerations. Only the person who knows God's presence and his promises has ultimate hope.

6. So, I have hope, since it continually remains true that "all things work together for the good of those who love God," even when we are prevented for much of the time from looking behind the curtains of suffering to see what is really going on. A woman with a son who was severely ill once said to me: "I keep hoping, because I know God doesn't make any mistakes."

7. I have hope, because God can do miracles when he wants to. In the letter to the Ephesians it says "God can do far more exceeding abundantly above all that we can ask for or even think of, so great is His power which is at work within us." Sometimes the miracle is already there in the fact that the individuals who are afflicted and their relatives do not succumb to bitter resignation.

8. I have hope because God loves and accepts individuals with psychiatric weaknesses, even if they cannot completely grasp this truth and express it in words.

9. I have hope, because God can even work through weakness. He pours His power into "earthly vessels" and says to the weak person: "my grace is all you need, because my power is made perfect in weakness."

10. Finally, I have hope, because our existence in this world is not to be compared with the eternal life which God promises to those who put their trust in him. Paul writes: "I consider that our present sufferings are not worth comparing with the glory that will be revealed in us."

It is my wish that this hopeful perspective may stimulate churches all over the world to explore in which way they can start caring for the mentally burdened, patients and families alike. This may start in changing the emphasis in preaching,[22] sensitizing the parish to the need of the suffering. And it could involve starting outreach to marginalized people in the community, working together with Christian teams of community health such as Emmanuel Hospital Fellowship, the Salvation Army and others. Several organizations are offering training material for nursing staff and lay people (e.g. www.BasicNeeds.org or courses by Prof. Vikram Patel in Goa). Although this article has been primarily focusing on developing countries, I have found a very helpful program for equipping the church at Saddleback Church in California. Their team has created an acronym, that encompasses the various steps in equipping the church:

---

[22] Moltmann, Power.

C — Care
H — Help
U — Unleash Volonteers
R — Reach out
C — Cooperation
H — Hope

The Gospel was not only written to warm our heart, but to call us to action. So if we want to bring health to needy people, let us remember: "There is no health without mental health!"

References

Antonowsky, A. (1979). Health, Stress and Coping. *The Jossey-Bass Social and Behavioral Science Series.*

Astbury, T & Tebboth, M. (2008). *Mental health and development: A model in practice.* Warwickshire, UK, BasicNeeds.

Benner, D. G. (1998). *Care of souls. Revisioning Christian nurture and counsel.* Grand Rapids, Mich.: Baker Books.

Bonelli, R. M., & Koenig, H. G. (June 01, 2013). Mental Disorders, Religion and Spirituality 1990 to 2010: A Systematic Evidence-Based Review. *Journal of Religion and Health*, 52(2), 657-673.

Cook, C., Powell, A., & Sims, A. C. P. (2009). *Spirituality and psychiatry.* London: Royal College of Psychiatrists.

Delitzsch, F., & Wallis, R. E. (1966). *A system of Biblical psychology.* Grand Rapids, Mich.: Baker Book House. Originally published in German: (1867). *System der biblischen Psychologie.* Edinburgh: T & T Clark.

Funk, M., Drew, N., Freeman, M., Faydi, E., World Health Organization. (2010). *Mental health and development: Targeting people with mental health conditions as a vulnerable group.* Geneva, Switzerland: World Health Organization. http://www.who.int/mental_health/policy/mh targeting /en/index.html

Gilbert, P. (2010). *Compassion focussed therapy: Distinctive Features.* London: Routledge.

Johnson, E.L. (2007). *Foundations for soul care. A Christian psychology proposal.* Downers Grove, Ill.: InterVarsity Press.

Kleinman A. (2009). Global mental health: a failure of humanity. *The Lancet*, Volume 374, Issue 9690.

Moltmann, J. (1983). *The power of the powerless.* San Francisco: Harper & Row.

Neufeld, V. (January 01, 1982). The Mennonite mental health story. *The Mennonite Quarterly Review*, 56(1), 18-31.

Pfeifer, S. (1994). Supporting the Weak. Christian Counselling and Contemporary Psychiatry. Word UK; free download as PDF: http://www.psy77.com/page/Tutorials.html

Prince M et al. (2007). No health without mental health. *The Lancet,* Vol. 370.

Patel V et al. (2003). The efficacy and cost-effectiveness of a drug and psychological treatment for common mental disorders in general health care in Goa, India: A randomised controlled trial. *The Lancet*, Vol. 361.

Raja S et al. (2008). *Evaluating Economic Outcomes of the Mental Health and Development Model in North India.* Warwickshire, UK, BasicNeeds.

Sharma D. (1999). Mental health patients face primitive conditions. *The Lancet,* Vol. 354.

Sims, A. C. P. (2009). *Is faith delusion? Why religion is good for your health.* London/New York: Continuum.

Srinivasa, M. R., Kishore, K. K. V., Chisholm, D., Thomas, T., Sekar, K., & Chandrashekari, C. R. (January 01, 2005). Community outreach for untreated schizophrenia in rural India: a follow-up study of symptoms, disability, family burden and costs. *Psychological Medicine*, 35(3), 341-51.

Vitz, P. C. (1977). *Psychology as religion. The cult of self-worship.* Grand Rapids: Eerdmans.

www.nurmanzil.org, [accessed Jan 19, 2014].

www.theretreatyork.org.uk, [accessed March 26, 2014].

Global Mental Health Needs and Consequences for Missions

Ulrich Giesekus

There are few statements about missions that are almost universally agreed on. One of them is the demand for mission to be holistic and address all areas of human need. It has been over 20 years that researchers have postulated that missions involves a significant amount of mental health work done by people who are not well equipped to deal with psychological disorders (Hesselgrave 1986). There is much evidence that over the 19 years since then, not much has changed. The *Cape Town Declaration* which was written during the 2010 Third International Congress at Cape Town, South Africa, again emphasizes the need for further attention to mental health issues:

> "... human conditions include different types and levels of social and psychological suffering which are often minimized, neglected or, because they are beyond what local people can cope with at a given time, left unattended or addressed from out-of-context perspectives. We believe these omissions are both unjust and costly to individuals and communities. Virtually all of the major public health problems in the world have a psychosocial component. There is no complete health without physical, communal and psychological health." (Smith et al., 2011)

It is obvious that poor training leads to ineffective helping and thus presents a disadvantage if not a danger to the counselees. Moreover, poor success, helplessness and treatment errors also lead to frustration and suffering for the helpers, possibly even being a health risk for them. It can be assumed that the mental hygiene aspect of good training for the helpers is significant.

Provided the helpers also have good intercultural skills, Western psychology and counseling skills can be used together with indigenous healing methods, rituals and ceremonies. There have been several examples of indigenous methods becoming an inspiration to Western pastoral counseling, e.g. David Seamands' (1981) approach "Healing for damaged emotions" which was developed during his missionary service in India. Examples of influences by indigenous methods on Western psychotherapy include the development of psychodrama, which was partly inspired by Pomo-Indian healing rituals (Moreno, 1959), reports of indigenous influences on creative therapies and dance and music-therapy (Aigen 1991), and similarities of network therapy approaches to indigenous Navajo ceremonies (Lee, 1999). The predominance of American Indian among the many indigenous influences may be due the fact that Western and Indian cultures interact more often. Intercultural psychosocial care is not a one-way-street and there are several ways in which training can be seen as a win-win-situation for missions.

Online Survey

In order to assess the psychosocial needs of developing countries, we used an online survey adapted from a previous version developed by Brad Smith and Lydia Bowen. This questionnaire was previously used in Ukrainian and English versions (cf., Ellens et al., 2000). Questions on trauma needs were added and the personal data section adjusted for the online process[1]. There are multiple choice and open answer sections which makes it possible to easily score the data while giving a possibility for individual answers. Both a German version and a revised English version were available.

The different sections of the survey include:

- Informed Consent
- Personal Data: Geographical area, profession, age, faith confession
- Which psychological disorders are most frequent?
- Who will be asked for help?
- Christian attitudes toward psychology within the region
- Appraisal: What is the best practice of counseling/psychotherapy in the region?
- Levels of helper training
- Need for further training

The Survey was distributed to international field workers working with Liebenzell Mission International. There were 44 returns (39 German, 5 English):

- 12 from Europe (work with migrant populations): Germany (3), Spain (3), France (3), Russia (2), Switzerland(1)
- 3 from Ecuador
- 15 from Africa: Zambia (7)*, Malawi (5)*[2], Burundi (3), Nigeria (1)
- 14 from Asia: Japan (5), Bangladesh (4), PNG (2), Kirgizstan (2), Pacific Islands (1)

---

[1] Many thanks to Nate Smith for his help in getting the survey into an online format and collecting the data.
[2] * One person answered for both countries

Results

In Table 1, I summarize the most important results of the survey:

The question, *"What are the most prominent mental health problems in your country?,"* yielded the following answers:

The Most Prominent Mental Health Problems

PROBLEM N=44	Never	Rarely	Sometimes	Often	Very often
Relationships	6	4	10	14	15
Marital problems	3	3	8	15	14
Drugs and alcohol	7	6	10	14	7
Domestic violence, abuse	9	11	16	9	4
Anxiety	4	13	15	10	2
Depression	6	12	14	10	2
Stress/burnout	5	13	17	9	0
Pornography/sex addiction	5	16	9	7	0
Sexual abuse	11	10	17	1	4
Trauma based on violence, war, i.e., caused by human behavior (n=19)	7	3	4	3	1
Severe mental disorders (psychotic, paranoid disorders, schizophrenia etc.)	12	22	7	2	0
Accidental trauma (n=19)	3	8	6	2	0
Eating disorders	18	14	10	1	0

Others:

Africa:
    Demon possession (indigenous population only), inferiority feelings, poor self-esteem.

Europe:
    Poverty, church conflict, isolation, suicide, (Spain, Germany, Russia, France, Switzerland).

Asia:
    Parent relationships, lack of vision, occult.

Table 1

These responses reflect personal impressions of frequent pathology and of course do not represent clinical diagnoses to standardized criteria such as defined by the Diagnostic and Statistical Manual of Mental Disorders (APA, 2013) or the International Statistical Classification of Diseases and Related Health Problems (WHO, 1992). Some diagnostic categories may in fact not be valid outside of Western cultures. So this does not necessarily reflect the actual pathology of a population, but the perception of problem areas by trained helpers from Western cultures.

Note that marital and relationship problems are clearly the number one concern. Depression, anxiety, stress/burnout, drug and alcohol abuse, domestic violence and sexual abuse are seen frequently, and, not surprisingly, eating disorders and psychotic disorders are not seen as frequently. Of course, a relatively small number of occurrences do not indicate that there is no concern, especially for the rare but serious disorders.

Which Attitudes and Beliefs do Christians in Your Country Have Toward Psychological Methods?

This was an open answer question. While 12 of the subjects reported that they didn't know any mental health services, the other answers can be combined into three categories:

- Rejection of psychological interventions or of the concept of mental disorder as a whole (22), such as "problems are God's punishment" or "Christians see their pastor, not a psychologist."
- Acceptance of only Christian mental health providers (6) or partial acceptance (3). In one case, Christian psychological speakers are seen as acceptable.
- Readiness to accept psychological help with high expectations (7).

The countries with high acceptance and expectations of mental health service among Christians are mostly European cultures and Japan. Not all of these responses were positive. For example, missionaries working in Swiss and German contexts considered the local Christian communities as hesitant in supporting Christian mental health work.

How is Christian Counseling Done?

The Christian workers in all non-Western cultures were very clear in their observation that Christian counseling is expected to be directive: the counselor solves the problems for the client. A typical example of these answers is: "The most common mode of counseling is: The people want to be told, what to do. The pastor knows what works, what is good or bad, and he tells the people—and either they do it or they don't." The numbers of sessions is limited to one or very few.

Only four missionaries reported that counselors are expected to facilitate the client's own initiative, self-reflective thinking, and one answer points out that family involvement is expected.

Clinical Training for Counselors

Another area of the survey refers to the clinical training that pastors or lay church workers have received. None of the pastors consider their own training to be "excellent," only eight as "sufficient," and clearly the largest portion have no (8) or little (27) training. The picture gets even worse when it comes to lay helpers and church staff. Twenty-seven reported that there was no training at all; 14 reported "little training," and none suggest there are sufficient or excellent training experiences.

Need for Further Training

The survey listed different types of counselor training and asked about the interest of the field workers in these (see Table 2, next page).

Again, marriage and education issues are clearly important. Christian academic training was seen as desirable for a large majority. Online support (via Skype, etc.), secular academic training, and practical training in clinics or institutions had the least interest. The little interest in online support was somewhat of a surprise to the author (who has frequently been asked by field workers for this service), but possibly, field workers do not expect that professionals in their home countries will have sufficient understanding of the dynamics of their host culture.

Legal Certification Requirements

In Western cultures, mental health services are frequently regulated and service providers have to attain licenses that prove sufficient training. In other parts of the world there is a great variation regarding licensing requirements. These requirements have to be considered when offering training or counseling services. The survey shows that even in regions where there is no mental health service available at all, licensure may apply (see Table 3, next page).

Types and Interest in Counselor Training

Type of training	Not interested	Little interest	Some interest	Lot of interest	Extremely interested
Seminars for marriage and family education	1	1	12	16	14
Clinical training	1	10	14	12	7
On-line training	6	11	10	8	9
Christian academic training	6	8	16	10	4
Mastercourse on Systemic Counseling (IHL)	8	11	9	7	3
Consultation via Skype etc. in dealing with mental disorders	9	13	13	7	2
Practicum in clinic/institution	8	15	13	5	1
Secular academic training	18	12	7	1	2

Table 2

The Importance of Licensing/Certification for Mental Health Workers

	Not at all	Generally not needed	Sometimes relevant	Important	Absolutely required
How important is state certification for mental health workers in your country?	2	7	13	11	5

Table 3

Integrative Approaches to Counseling

The validity of Western psychological constructs in diverse cultural contexts is questionable. What would seem a symptom of a serious disorder in one context may be quite normal within another culture. If a typical German were to nail an animal's foot to his door frame to defend his family from evil curses and keep the family healthy, he would likely be considered mentally ill. In other parts of the world, this might not at all be the case. Intercultural psychosocial care needs paradigms in which culture itself is seen as a context in which cultural and individual realities are constructed. Cultural history and its meaning for everyday life, communication rules, definitions of normality and of disturbance, familial norms and structures, and emotional experiences, to name a few aspects, can be very different across cultures. Understanding not only the client's culture as such a system, but even more so the counselor's own personal values, thinking, feeling and behaving as culturally defined, is extremely important. The history of missions and economic development efforts contain too many elements of culture-insensitive, top-down approaches, often causing damage to the people one wants to serve. A systemic paradigm is generally helpful in intercultural counseling, as systems theory places an emphasis on the context in which human life takes place. Beyond that, integrative approaches value indigenous methods and traditional wisdom, as well as traditional Christian pastoral care. The integration of interculturally-sensitive approaches, psychological Western science, indigenous methods and Christian faith goes beyond any existing framework of mental health counseling.

Theses

A small and limited survey can only be preliminary and yield tentative conclusions more than definitive results. However, on the basis of previous research and the results of our survey, I have formulated 12 theses with which I will end:

1. In many regions of the world there is an urgent need for mental health services.

2. Mental health is a significant problem in developing countries.

3. Help is expected from religious/spiritual sources.

4. Christian counselors in the majority world have to be holistic in their approach. The reality of the invisible and visible world must be acknowledged and considered in practice.

5. Relationship counseling is a significant emphasis in the majority world.

6. Psychopathology, trauma, addiction, violence, etc. are frequent problems and require clinical competencies.

7. Intercultural counseling requires intercultural competence. Western paradigms of counseling contribute important aspects but are not sufficient.

8. Intercultural counseling requires systemic approaches since the context defines most interpersonal processes.

9. Intercultural counseling requires good theological competence, since spiritual aspects are part of all systems and are therefore more likely emphasized.

10. Indigenous methods of healing are not all occult or primitive, but on the contrary, the resources from the context need to be integrated in helping approaches. Counseling "against the culture" will not be accepted or effective.

11. Missions, and church workers, are not sufficiently trained in areas of clinical work, mental health counseling or marriage and family counseling.

12. There is little research on the integration of Western "scientific" psychology with a Christian world view, as well as indigenous, traditional methods of healing. Scientific study in these areas is one of the challenges for future mission work.

Conclusion

This study is a preliminary assessment of mental health needs based on the impressions of a small number of field workers from very different regions. The numbers are not sufficient to conduct a statistical analysis of regional differences, even though these differences are obviously extremely likely (e.g., the mental health needs of Japan and Ecuador are not likely identical).

The impressions of the field workers are not identical to the real needs. People who are not trained to recognize clinical disorders such as depression or anxiety disorders are likely to underreport these problems, whereas marriage and parenting issues may be over-reported, since family issues are more often the focus of previous training experiences.

Also, the perception of mental health needs are likely somewhat dependent on the observer's own attitudes and beliefs about psychological methods. Similarly, their view of the indigenous Christian culture is likely to be partly dependent on the field workers own attitudes and beliefs. We have not asked regarding the mission workers' own attitudes and assume that Liebenzell Mission workers do not generally object to integrating psychological science.

The response rate is unclear as the online link to the survey was freely distributed among international field workers employed by the Liebenzell Mission. It is quite possible that psychologically disinterested staff have not answered the survey all together, thus skewing the results toward the more psychologically minded workers.

Further research is needed. There is a strong indication that mental health needs are significant and psychological competencies are needed and desired; however, it is unclear how representative these results are. All in all, the results can be considered as evidence that the synthesis and integration of theological, intercultural, clinical and systemic competencies should become a central emphasis in training, continuing education and support for mission and church workers in the developing world.

References

Aigen, K. (1991). *The roots of music therapy: Towards an indigenous research paradigm.* (Doctoral Dissertation, New York Univ.) UMI order #9134717. http://steinhardt.nyu.edu/scmsAdmin/uploads/005/496/AigenKen1991.pdf

American Psychiatric Association (APA; 2013). *Diagnostic and statistics manual of mental disorders* (5th ed.). Washington, DC: APA.

Bowen, D. (2008, July). The need for field-based counselor training in evangelical missions. *Evangelical Missions Quarterly.* Retrieved from http://www.emqonline.com/emq/issue-304/2159.

Chang, R. (2007). *Successful cross-cultural teamwork: Definitions, structures, conclusions.* Saarbrücken, Germany: VDM Verlag Dr. Mueller.

Dueck, A., & Reimer, K. (2009). *A peaceable psychology: Christian therapy in a world of many cultures.* Grand Rapids, MI: Brazos.

Ellens, B., McMinn, M., Lake, L., Hardy, M., & Hayden, E. (2000). A preliminary assessment of mental health needs faced by religious leaders in Eastern Europe. *Journal of Psychology and Theology, 28(1)*, 54–63.

Hegemann, T., & Oestereich, C. (2009). *Einführung in die interkulturelle systemische Beratung und Therapie.* Heidelberg, Germany: Auer.

Hesselgrave, D. (1986). Culture-sensitive counseling and the Christian mission. *International Bulletin of Missionary Research, 10*, 109–116.

Hofstede, G. (2001). *Culture's consequences: Comparing values, behaviors, institutions and organizations across nations* (2nd ed.). Thousand Oaks, CA: Sage.

Lee, W. (1999). *An Introduction to multicultural counseling.* Philadelphia, PA: Taylor & Francis.

Levant, R. F. (1984). *Family therapy: A comprehensive overview.* Englewood Cliffs, NJ: Prentice-Hall.

Moreno, J. L. (1959). *Gruppenpsychotherapie und Psychodrama. Einführung in die Theorie und Praxis.* Stuttgart, Germany: Thieme.

Mwiti, G., & Dueck, A. (2006). *Christian counselling: An African indigenous perspective.* Pasadena, CA: Fuller Seminary Press.

Schlippe, A., El Hachimi, M., & Jürgens, G. (2013). *Multikulturelle systemische Praxis.* Heidelberg, Germany: Auer.

Seamands, D. (1981). *Healing for damaged emotions.* Colorado Springs, CO: David C. Cook.

Smith, B., Collins, G. R., Cruz, E., Cruz, P., Cruz, S., Cruz Jr., S., Dueck, A., Gingrich, F., Hughes, D., Mwiti, G., Vuncannon, J., & Warlow, J. (2011). *The Cape Town declaration on care and counsel as mission.* Retrieved from www.careandcounsel.org.

World Health Organization (WHO; 1992). *International statistical classification of diseases and related health problems (ICD;* 10th ed.). Retrieved from http://apps.who.int/classifications/icd10/browse/2016/en.

African Americans and Mental Health: Challenges and Church-Based Responses

Bradford M. Smith and Kathryn A. Cummins

Introduction

As we are considering the role of the global church in mental health this week we have emphasized the role of culture and context in addressing needs. In this paper, we would like to describe an emerging initiative in Jackson, Mississippi, USA, the capital city of one of the poorest states in the US. In particular we will focus on the role and potential of the African American Church in addressing the underserved population of African Americans who comprise approximately 80 percent of the Jackson population. We hope to demonstrate the importance of understanding the unique history of particular ethnic groups, the impact of their socioeconomic status, and other sociocultural variables that shape both the nature of the need and the resources available in providing adequate mental health care.

Within this past year my wife, Amy and I (Brad) have moved from Boston, Massachusetts to Jackson, Mississippi as part of this initiative. We were both invited to positions at Belhaven University, Amy to teach in the nursing department and me to teach in the psychology department and to start the Institute for International Care and Counsel. This meant I was leaving my counseling private practice in Boston of over twenty years to pursue this vision of mobilizing and equipping churches worldwide to address the serious mental health needs of their people and communities.

When we got to Jackson and began to understand more deeply the context of Mississippi through the lens of my thinking on global mental health and the church, I faced an ethical challenge: I could not think only globally and ignore the local needs that were in my own neighborhood. This realization led to further exploration, prayer, discussion, and ultimately the formation of this current project of working collaboratively with African American churches to explore possible collaboration for strengthening their role in the mental health of their communities.

Mental health is increasingly being recognized as a serious issue facing our world. It has historically been misunderstood both inside and outside churches and not always addressed in helpful ways. There are still major disparities between: (1) the attention given mental health compared to other public health issues, (2) the health of people with mental illness compared to those without this challenge, and (3) different populations with respect to mental health and the quality, accessibility, and outcomes of care. Matthew 9:36 says when Jesus "saw the crowds, he had compassion on them because they were confused and helpless." God is allowing the global Church to see the tremendous needs of people, including their mental health needs, in a clearer, more complete way. There is a great opportunity for churches to be at the forefront of addressing mental health support needs through raising awareness, providing hope and support, and connecting individuals, congregations, and communities with needed resources. However, as we move forward, it is important that our strategies and programs be sensitive and appropriate to the particular cultural and community context.

The African American community in the U.S. faces particular disparities and is in need of dramatically improved services. African Americans make up approximately 15 percent of the US population. In Mississippi, 38.1% of the population is Black, and in Jackson, the capital where we now live, the Black population is 79.4%. Mississippi ranks last among the U.S. states in many categories related to quality of life, such as education, health, poverty, and life expectancy. The state finished fifth worst on Gallup-Healthways Well-Being Index (2014), which takes into account multiple quality of life indicators such as emotional and physical health, financial opportunity and security, and community support and safety. In addition, such public comparative rankings have contributed to frequent attitudes of shame, inferiority and defensiveness within the people of the state.

Mental health problems can have an insidious impact on many areas of overall wellbeing. In all of the issues facing Mississippi, mental illness plays a significant but often unrecognized role. The influence of mental health reaches out into the community beyond physical health and impacts social issues such as:

- Youth, families, and communities — There is a complex, multidirectional relationship between mental health problems and other issues facing youth, families, and communities such as divorce, child custody issues, safety and violence. Mental illness is commonly triggered early in life. Half of all long-term mental illness begins by age fourteen and three quarters by age twenty-four (NAMI, 2014). Nearly 35,000 of Mississippi's children and youth have severe and persistent mental health needs, which can impact every aspect of their lives (Mississippi Department of Mental Health, n.d.). In a report released by the Annie E. Casey Foundation (n.d.), Mississippi ranks 50th out of the fifty US states in terms of the four domains of child well-being indicators: (1) economic well-being, (2) education, (3) health, and (4) family and community.

- Mental illness and homelessness — Approximately twenty-six percent of adults in homeless shelters live with serious mental illness and an estimated forty-six percent live with severe mental illness and/or substance use disorders (NAMI, n.d.). According to the National Coalition for the Homeless (2009), African Americans comprise forty percent of all homeless people.

- Mental illness and the criminal justice system — In 2013, Mississippi had a rate of incarcerated adults per 100,000 about seventy-five percent higher than the national average. In addition, like every other state in the U.S., Mississippi incarcerates more individuals with severe mental illness than it hospitalizes (National Institute of Corrections and Treatment Advocacy Center, 2010). Many people with mental illness rotate in and out of the criminal justice system frequently for small, nonviolent crimes (NAMI, n.d.). Correctional facilities are not properly equipped to handle the needs of these individuals. Court systems are unprepared to deal with mental health issues and people with mental illness fail to receive the treatment they need in jails and prisons.

- Mental health and missed work — Mental illness is among the biggest drivers of healthcare costs and reduced worker productivity. Full-time employees in the United States with depression miss nearly twice as many workdays each year than those employees who have never been depressed. On a national scale, this means depression is linked with 68 million absences from work each year, translating to an estimated $23 billion in lost productivity for employers (Gallop, 2013).

Mental Health Disparities and African Americans

As noted above, the term "mental health disparities" can be understood in three categories: disparities between the attention given mental health versus other public health issues, the health of individuals with mental illness compared with that of those without, and between different populations with respect to mental health and the quality, accessibility, and outcomes of care.

In the case of African American communities, the types of barriers that interfere with accessing mental health services include the lack of culturally competent care, geographic inaccessibility, lack of medical insurance, and a "double stigma" resulting from racism and prejudice, and a distrust of medical professionals. To understand the mental health of African Americans, it is necessary to recognize the unique historical context of slavery and exclusion from social, economic, and educational opportunities that continues to impact their psychological health and well-being today (U.S. Department of Health and Human Services, 2001).

An episode of unethical medical research that significantly undermined African American's trust in the U.S. health care system was the infamous "Tuskegee Study of Untreated Syphilis in the Negro Male." In 1932, there was a research initiative started based on the hypothesis that syphilis had different effects among African Americans than whites. The study was to last six months but instead lasted forty years. It involved 600 African American men, 399 who had syphilis, 201 who did not. Without providing a complete informed consent, these 399 infected men were led to believe that they would receive treatment for their disease but they did not. Even in 1945 when penicillin became recognized as a treatment of choice for syphilis, the men received no treatment and the decision was made, without their input, to follow their course of the syphilis disease until they died. It was not until 1969 that this surfaced into public awareness. In 1972 financial reparations were made to the men who were alive and to their families. In 1997 then President Bill Clinton officially apologized on behalf of the nation to these men and their families. In light of this particular ethical breach, it is evident that besides the historical atrocities of slavery, repression, and physical violence, there is reason for distrust by African Americans towards the health care system.

The long history of racism has caused the African American community to look inwards for survival, support, purpose, guidance, and aid. This has produced strong community resilience and collective thinking. However, in the area of mental health, there are many instances of misunderstanding, misdiagnosis and improper treatment of individuals by mental health professionals. Not surprisingly, there are also negative preconceived notions about professionals and helpers by African American individuals and communities. Especially in minority communities, the obstacles to getting individuals the assistance they need comes from both sides of the helping relationship. These realities must be taken into consideration as one approaches working and helping. It exemplifies the need for culturally-specific approaches to mental health needs in different communities.

There are well documented mental health disparities in prevalence of disorders, quality of treatment, and access to treatment. For example, even though African Americans have lower lifetime rates of major depressive disorder than non-Hispanic white Americans (Breslau, Kendler, Su, Gaxiola-

Aguilar, & Kessler, 2005), African Americans with major depressive disorder are more impaired and more persistently ill (Williams et al., 2007). There are questions as to the accuracy of diagnosis of African Americans especially given the lack of African American clinicians. For example, African Americans are twice as likely as non-Hispanic whites to be diagnosed with schizophrenia (American Psychological Association, 2016). Meanwhile, there is serious concern about the cultural competence of treaters given, for example, that less than two percent of American Psychological Association members are Black/African American (American Psychological Association, 2014).

Stigma and judgment are another problem that can prevent African Americans from seeking treatment. Many African Americans believe they would be viewed as "crazy" by their friends or family if they admitted to symptoms of depression or anxiety (Williams, 2011). There are disparities in rates of treatment as well. For example, in 2011, 54.3% of adult Black/African Americans with a major depressive episode received treatment, compared with 73.1% of adult white Americans (Williams, 2011).

The Role of the Church in African American Society

Religion, church communities, and pastors, play a central role in African American culture. According to PEW Research Center (2009), religion is more important to African Americans than to the US population as a whole. 79% of African American adults versus 56% of all other US adults say religion is very important. The church community plays a central, comprehensive, and holistic role in the life of African American people. It is quite common for African American churches to be involved in issues of social justice, housing, job training, and physical health. Church-based Health Promotion Programs (CBHPP), have been used to target such health issues as cancer, diabetes, HIV and AIDS, obesity and weight loss, cardiovascular disease and hypertension, and asthma in the Black Church. In light of all of this, Hankerson and Weissman (2012) concluded that the Black Church is being underutilized as a potential mental health resource.

Disparities, as those discussed above, as well as the potential of faith communities as resources have drawn the attention of researchers and foundations. In 2014, the Hogg Foundation for Mental Health (University of Texas at Austin, 2014) awarded $946,600 in grants over three years to eleven faith-based organizations in Texas to increase awareness and perceptions of mental health, recovery, and wellness in African American communities. The goals of this initiative are to build on the unique strengths of churches and other faith-based organizations in African American communities to identify and connect congregants with local behavioral resources for treatment and support. An additional goal is to support faith leaders in addressing their own mental wellness.

In 2012, Hankerson and Weissman conducted an extensive literature review on the role of African American churches in mental health, focusing on eight research articles based of projects that were conducted in the church and met established research standards. In areas of smoking cessation, cocaine abuse, depressive and anxiety symptoms, and substance use prevention programs, effective studies utilized elements particularly relevant to the African American spiritual experience by employing church-based coalitions, training, and programs, devotional booklets, counseling, mentorship, group support, prayer, etc.

One example of particular interest is a comprehensive model known as PEWS: Promoting Emotional Wellness and Spirituality (Williams, Gorman & Hankerson, 2014), which utilizes Community-based Participatory Research (CBPR). The PEWS program which was implemented in a locality in the state of New Jersey in the U.S., was formed from an advisory group composed of community stakeholders and participants and began with two spirituality and wellness conferences with a combined attendance of 400 to raise community awareness and provide an initial rallying place. They also produced a ten hour training curriculum designed to assist churches in either expanding their current health ministry to include a mental health dimension or developing a free-standing mental health ministry committee (Williams, Gorman, & Hankerson, 2014). This model included important strategies such as seeking out community leadership and support and utilizing positive terminology, such as wellness and discipleship.

In summarizing their approach, Williams, Gorman, & Hankerson made the following recommendations:

1. Form partnerships with church leaders and staff if there was not an existing relationship with the senior pastor.

2. Use an inclusive, collaborative approach with the goal of building trusting relationships.

3. Be flexible in what format is used for providing training to churches.

An Emerging Project: The Mississippi Faith-Based Health and Mental Health Initiative

Based on our review of the above literature, Belhaven University's Institute for International Care and Counsel is launching a new initiative closely following the model of the PEWS project. An important guiding principle for us is to regard this effort as an ongoing initiative rather than a one-time conference event. We envision this initiative in three phases.

Phase 1 will be a needs assessment phase where we will use qualitative methods such as individual interviews and focus groups to hear from local churches and others in the community about the needs and resources that currently exist in the area of mental health. We are seeking to hear from key stakeholders in the community. Besides gathering information, an important benefit from this work will be building relationships and trust within the community. We anticipate participants will include: pastors, mental health workers, faith community nurses, parachurch ministry workers, public safety officers, health ministers, other health professionals, community agencies, students, educators, and consumers.

Phase 2 will be a one and a half day *Summit on the Church, Health, and Mental Health* where we will gather key stakeholders in the community. The goals of the Summit will be:

1. *Raise awareness* in the community about the often unseen, devastating effects of mental illness, its close connection to overall health and well-being, and its significant contribution to other more visible personal, social, and economic problems.

2. *Connect stakeholders* including pastors, faith community nurses, health ministries, mental health professionals, health professionals and community and governmental agencies around this issue.

3. *Develop* a common understanding and knowledge of the needs and resources available and the potential for collaboration from a community systems perspective.

4. *Identify and implement next steps for moving forward together* through sustainable initiatives.

Phase 3 will be the launching of ongoing initiatives based on the priorities and agenda established in the Summit. Anticipated outcomes include future training, functional networks, and assisting churches in the development of health and mental health programs and partnerships.

Summary

This paper has been a case study on challenges and approaches to enhancing mental health care in the city of Jackson, Mississippi, which is almost eighty percent African American. Cultural factors and the historical background of the African American community have been noted as key factors. In this particular community, the central roles of the church, and especially pastors, have been emphasized.

We believe that developing higher levels of engagement of churches in the area of mental health, wherever in the world it takes place, is very local, contextualized work. Congregations uniquely reflect and affect their particular communities. The history of the people involved is important, along with identifying and addressing both particular strengths and challenges of a population. Research is a key component. Participatory research techniques can build relationship and trust. As potential helpers, we must come in a spirit of humility and enter into a community with a desire to collaborate, learn, and respect the wishes of the community itself realizing that sustainable change will only come from the support of the community. Our hope is that this paper will provide guiding principles for contextualizing mental health care in under-served contexts around the world.

References

American Psychological Association. (2014). Demographic characteristics of APA members by membership characteristics. Retrieved from http://www.apa.org/workforce/publications/14-member/table-1.pdf.

American Psychological Association. (2016). African Americans have limited access to mental and behavioral health care. Retrieved from http://www.apa.org/about/gr/issues/minority/access.aspx.

Annie E. Casey Foundation (n.d.). Retrieved from http://datacenter.kidscount.org/data#MS/2/0/char/.

Breslau, J., Kendler, K.S., Su, M., Gaxiola-Aguilar, S., & Kessler, R.C. (2005). Lifetime risk and persistence of psychiatric disorders across ethnic groups in the United States. *Psychological Medicine, 35(3)*, 317–327.

Gallup-Healthways (2014). *Well-Being Index*. Retrieved from http://www.well-beingindex.com/2014-state-rankings.

Hankerson, S.H. & M. Weissman (2012). Church-based health programs for mental disorders among African Americans: A review. *Psychiatric Services. 63(3)*, 243–249.

Mississippi Department of Mental Health (n.d.). Children and Youth Services. Retrieved from http://www.dmh.ms.gov/service-options/mental-heal th/children-and-youth-services/.

National Alliance on Mental Illness (n.d.). Mental health by the numbers. Retrieved from http://www.nami.org/Learn-More/Mental-Health-By-the-Numbers.

National Alliance on Mental Illness (2014). State Mental Health Legislation 2014. Trends, Themes & Effective Practices. Retrieved from http://www.nami.org/legreport2014.

National Coalition for the Homeless (2009, July). Minorities and homelessness. Retrieved from http://www.nationalhomeless.org/factsheets/mi norities.html.

National Institute of Corrections and Treatment Advocacy Center (2010). Criminalization of mental illness in Mississippi. Retrieved from http://www.treatmentadvocacycenter.org/mississippi.

Pew Research Center (2009, January 30). A religious portrait of African-Americans. Retrieved from http://www.pewforum.org/2009/01/30/a-religious-portrait-of-african-americans/.

University of Texas at Austin (2014, November 25). Hogg Foundation Awards $946,600 in Grants to Faith-Based Organizations for Mental Health Education in African American Communities. Retrieved from http://diversity.utexas.edu/news/2014/11/25/hogg-foundation-awa rds-946600-in-grants-to-faith-based-organizations-for-mental-health-education-in-african-american-communities/.

U.S. Department of Health and Human Services (2001). Mental health: Culture, race, and ethnicity: A supplement to mental health: A report of the surgeon general. Retrieved from https://www.ncbi.nlm.nih.gov/books/NBK44251/#A1415.

Willen, L. (2012, July 27). Mississippi learning: Why the state's students start behind—and stay behind. *The Hechinger Report.* Retrieved from http://content.time.com/time/nation/article/0,8599,2120539,00.html.

Williams, D.R., Gonzalez, H.M., Neighbors, H.M., Nesse, R. Ableson, J.M., Sweetman, J., & Jackson, J.S. (2007). Prevalence and distribution of major depressive disorder in African Americans, Caribbean blacks, and non-Hispanic whites: Results from the National Survey of American Life. *Archives of General Psychiatry, 64(3)*, 305–315.

Williams, L., Gorman R., & S.H. Hankerson (2014). Implementing a mental health ministry committee in faith-based organizations: The Promoting Emotional Wellness and Spirituality Program. *Social Work in Health Care. 53(4)*, 414–434.

Witters, D., Lieu, D., & Agrawal, S. (2013, July 24). Depression costs U.S. workplaces $23 billion in absenteeism. Retrieved from http://www.gallup.com/poll/163619/depression-costs-workplaces-billion-absenteeism.aspx.

Sickness and Healing in an Animistic Context

Simon Herrmann

Introduction

People's ideas and beliefs about sickness are not the same everywhere, nor are the ways how they deal with sickness. People who live in animistic contexts look at the world they live in from a certain perspective, often peculiar to people from the West. This article seeks to inform those who work with people with animistic backgrounds. It also seeks to offer advice from a Christian perspective about how to minister to such people meaningfully.

In a first part, I will introduce the main aspects of animism that are important for the topic under discussion. In the second part I will illustrate how people deal with sickness in an animistic context, based on the example of the Lele people of Manus Island, Papua New Guinea. This where I have lived and worked with my family since 2006 and where I am currently carrying out research that is closely related to the topic of this article. In part three, I will offer five points for consideration from a Christian perspective for those who work among people with an animistic understanding of the world.

The two following real-life stories provide a first glimpse into the world of the Lele people. They illustrate some of the aspects of life that are of relevance for them in times of calamity.

First story: Nicky's diabetes

Nicky[1], a Christian in his early fifties and a former chairman of the local church was sick with diabetes. He was about to lose one of his toes as a consequence of it. When it all began, he went to the hospital as most people would do in such a situation. However, the doctors there were not able to help him. While he was still at the hospital, three people came to him, independently of each other. They all told him the same thing: "Nicky, this sickness is not a sickness!" Nicky had not asked them to come; they came to see him and told him that his sickness was not "just" diabetes. (What they actu-

---

[1] All names have been changed in order to protect the persons' privacy.

ally meant by this was that his sickness was not that kind of sickness that can be treated at the hospital. It had another, underlying cause which the hospital was simply not competent in treating.) They also said that they "saw" how some people put "something" in his car, near the accelerator pedal. Based on the message of these three people, Nicky was convinced: "They got me with ginger!" (Ginger, as everyone on Manus knows, is one of the means people use for sorcery.) For the people it was clear: Someone had used sorcery to harm Nicky and diabetes was just the symptom of it.

Nicky went back to his house and a traditional healer came to see him. He said: "Let me see your toe! I can spit at your toe, using ginger." (The idea is that the ginger carries the power of the spirits). He offered that Nicky should eat some of the ginger and he himself would chew it and then spit at the toe. The healer also told him, that Nicky would "see" a picture in his mind that would reveal more details about the cause of the sickness when he accepted the treatment. Nicky did not really believe in what the healer was offering. But as he was already there with him and he knew him well, he gave it a try. So he let him spit at the toe. The treatment was not effective and eventually the toe was amputated.

Second story: Susan's barrenness

Susan got married a couple of years ago. At the ceremony, her father gave the groom's family a huge pig but only received a very small amount of money in return. He was very upset and said to his daughter: "You will only carry firewood and water on your back, but no children!" The couple remained without children for seven years. Her husband was beating Susan many times because he suspected that she was using contraceptives and did not want to have children with him. He was about to send her back to her family. Then she remembered the curse and told her husband about it.

They went back to her father, brought him a gift, and reconciled with him. Her father said: "Go into the kitchen, leave some oil there and wait for me. Later I will come to perform a ritual to reverse the curse." At nighttime he came, rubbed her back with the oil, touched her with some leaves and uttered some words to take back the curse. Within a few weeks she was pregnant.

The two stories show that these people conceptualize their world in different ways than most people who grew up in the Western world. Nevertheless, for the people there, this is part of the world they live in and it is part of what they would describe as reality. For cross-cultural workers it takes time to dig into these issues and learn how people understand their lives, their relationships, and the world they live in.

Basics of Animistic Beliefs

The term animism is often connected with "the belief that inanimate objects and natural phenomena have souls" (Morris, 2012, 10).[2] For this article, I want to follow Hiebert, Shaw, and Tiénou (1999, 76) and use the term in a broader sense, referring to "the beliefs and practices associated with the 'middle zone,' with this-worldly supernatural realities such as earthly spirits, magic, evil eye, divination, and the like." Within an animistic paradigm, certain practices make sense for the people, even if they are difficult to be comprehended by outsiders.

It is characteristic of animistic beliefs and practices that they are focused on the here and now; they are this-worldly centered. People are more concerned with finding a good life than with upholding and defending certain principles as truth. Animistic practices therefore have a pragmatic orientation; whatever brings about the desired effect, is considered good. In traditional Papua New Guinea culture, the greatest aim is to have a good life, which consist of "security, health, wealth, growth, prestige, good relationships" and is not hindered by "sickness, decay, barrenness, [and] death" (Mantovani, 1998, 5). The good life is thereby always experienced in community with others. Not the individual is at the center, but the clan. In order to be able to live a good life on earth, one must consider the wider environment which includes the unseen world.

The Middle Zone[3]

Religious people in the Western world are commonly looking at two levels of reality: On one level there is the seen world (with everything that can be sensed, technology, science …), and on the other the spiritual world (God). God is seen as important for a purpose in life, for final destination, as highest moral instance, and maybe for forgiveness of sin. But everything else has to do with the seen world, with what can be touched, seen, "known." There is not much room for anything in between.[4]

For people with animistic beliefs, on the other hand, there is a lot of room between the seen world and the unseen world of high religions. This is

---

[2] For the historical developments of the term "animism", see part I of Harvey (2006). For an excellent introduction to animism see Käser (2004); now also available in English (2014).
[3] The presentation here is based on Hiebert (1982).
[4] This is of course an oversimplified representation. Especially with the influx of New Age movements and the influence of Eastern religions many people have developed a new openness for the spiritual world and the unseen realm.

called the "middle zone." Animists do not deny the existence of the seen world and most of these societies have an understanding of a highest being. This highest being created the world and the people, but is now often understood as being far away and not really concerned with the affairs of the world and even less with people's daily lives. What really matters is the middle zone where shamans and magic, ancestors and spirits, cursing and blessing are of relevance. This middle zone is important in three ways:

- Here, the *uncertainties of the future* are dealt with. This is where people look for help to prevent accidents, to find success, to ensure a happy marriage, etc. People look for someone who knows what the future holds and who has (or is believed to have) power to manipulate what happens.
  The remarks of a man on Manus I recently talked to, illustrates this well. He said: "If I need a loan from the bank but I have doubts that the bank grants it, I will go to someone who has the power to make it happen. He will take a leaf from a certain brush, put some knots in it and utter a spell which will cause the bank director to be in favor of my request."

- There are also *crises and uncertainties of the present life*. People get sick, the crops in the garden do not grow well, women do not get pregnant or students fail in their education. Many people in the Western world would locate the causes and look for help in the seen world: they fertilize the garden, build a dam to regulate the flow of water, or take extra lessons in school. People in an animistic context, however, usually focus on the middle zone, both for the causes and the remedies. For example, as in Susan's case in the introductory story, they take into account that a curse could be the underlying problem of barrenness and that the one who spoke it needs to reverse it in order for a woman to get pregnant. Or they put magic sticks in the ground at the corners of a garden to prevent wild pigs from destroying it.

- In addition, there are the *unanswered questions of the past*: Who stole my pig? Why did my child die so early? Who or what caused me to get sick? Again, people with an animistic orientation focus on the middle zone. While many people in the West would attribute hardship to chance, inadvertency, or evil people, in animistic contexts, mediums or shamans are often consulted to receive answers, guidance and help from the unseen world.

For the discussion of sickness and healing, to be aware of this middle zone (which is of little importance in Western and of great importance in animistic contexts) is essential.

Many people in the West focus on the seen world for the causes and remedies of sickness. If someone has the flu, most people in the West would expect that they caught it by way of contagion and look for medicine to treat it. For people with an animistic orientation, cause and effect are often to be sought in the middle zone, which, although part of the unseen world, is still very closely connected with people's daily lives. Even if they are aware of bacteria and viruses and other ways to get sick, many people would still ask: Who wanted me to get sick? What is the underlying cause that I got sick? This deeper, underlying cause is usually anchored in the middle zone.

Folk Religion

When formal religions (like Christianity or Islam) meet animistic beliefs and practices, the two often mingle. The term "folk religion" is used to describe "animistic beliefs and practices that are adapted into one of the formal world religions" (Morgan, 2012,).

It raises missiological concern if animistic beliefs are incorporated without reflection into the Christian faith. The outcome is a "split-level" Christianity (Hiebert, Shaw, & Tiénou, 1999, 14) where people need Christ for the ultimate questions but use their traditional systems to find help for their daily needs. Christ and the Church, then, have nothing to contribute to people's ordinary lives. This is not the vision of Jesus who called people to become his followers. Gladys Mwiti, during this symposium mentioned the danger that "we help people to go to heaven, but we do not help them to live on earth" (paraphrased).

Conceptions of Sickness and Healing among the Lele of Manus Island, Papua New Guinea

This section provides a case study from the Lele people on Manus Island, Papua New Guinea and reflects their understanding of sickness and healing. It is not representative of all animistic cultures, but provides an insight in how these specific people understand sickness and how they deal with it.[5]

---

[5] The data comes from research I conducted with seers and traditional healers from among the Lele and a survey among the general population to validate the findings. The research was carried out as part of my doctoral studies between July 2014 and July 2015.

Causes of Sickness

The Lele speak of what they call "normal" or "natural" causes of sickness. They have a basic understanding of contagion and know that malaria, for example, is transmitted by mosquitos. Most people do have access to basic health care. When they receive medicine at the local aid post or the small hospital and the sickness disappears, no further questions are being asked. Some people also think of this kind of sickness to be sent by God. God is understood to work through the public health system and if a sickness can be treated effectively in this way, it was probably God who had sent the sickness, because he also provided the remedy.

Then, there are sicknesses people themselves are responsible for. One example are people who worry too much, cannot find peace and therefore get sick. Another example are people who have smoked marijuana. If they are mentally affected, people do not look for the reasons in the middle zone. They know that the consumption of marijuana has negative consequences on one's health.

Then, there are sicknesses that people see caused by spirits that are connected to the natural world. People believe that in the crown of huge trees there sit small dwarfs. At the time of sunset, the dwarfs are looking for small children. If someone passes by with a child on his or her back, the dwarf would come and snatch the soul of the little child and the child would get sick. There are other spirit-beings that live at waterfalls, huge rocks or caves. They also can harm people and make them sick.

Another cause for sickness is cursing. The words in and of themselves are believed to have power. In the understanding of the Lele, there are no spirit-beings involved when people are cursed. If the curse is spoken by the right person, it will bring about the desired outcome.

Further, it is possible that someone asked the ancestors to send sickness. There is a clear distinction between spirits that are connected to the natural world and the spirits of the deceased. The spirits of the deceased are believed to be near and they can cause harm for the living. If someone harvested fruits in the garden of someone else, that person could go to the grave of a deceased relative and say: "You know, XY has stolen my banana. He did me evil. Go, and make him sick!"

The ancestors who look after the clan can also take the initiative themselves and cause someone in the clan to become sick. If they see division and want the clan to be united again, they might single out one person, make that person sick, and so bring people together to speak about their grievances against each other and settle their quarrels. This is believed to be a presupposition for the sick person's health to be restored.

Another reason for sickness is that if someone has died an unnatural death, the blood (i.e., the spirit) of that person will "jump" onto those who come near the place where the person had died. As a consequence, people either get mentally disturbed or develop a skin disease.

Lastly, it is possible that someone used sorcery against someone else and this caused the person to get sick. Sorcery can take many forms, e.g. lime that is loaded with the power of the spirits is mixed into someone's food and if the person, unaware of the manipulation that has taken place, eats it, that person will get sick.

Finding the Cause of a Sickness

The steps undertaken to cure a sickness are also means to find out what caused the sickness. Usually people use the public health care system (aid posts, the hospital, physicians and nurses, medicine that is dispensed by health professionals). If the sickness can be treated successfully, people do not inquire any further.

But if this does not work out, they would usually call the family together and ask: "Are there any quarrels, is there any disunity among us? Has someone undertaken steps to make the person sick (like calling upon the ancestors to do so)? Is there anything that stands between us so that we have to reconcile, unite again, and with that deal with the cause of the sickness?"

If this step remains inconclusive, they would go and find a specialist in order to seek help. In the understanding of the Lele, it is very likely that in such cases there is a spiritual dimension to the sickness and the sickness has to be combatted by dealing with the spirits who caused it. People would then go to the diviner. The diviner "looks" into the unseen world to figure out what caused the person to get sick. One method some diviners use is to chew betel-nut together with betel pepper and lime. The mixture makes the salivia red. They roll a leaf, bite off a piece, unroll the leaf and then "read" the cause of the sickness from the pattern the red saliva produced on the leaf.[6] Some-

---

[6] There are also some other methods. Someone told me that when his blood "shoots" in a certain body part this indicates what caused someone to get sick. These methods of divination are not only used for finding the cause of a sickness, but for many areas of life where people try to find help or guidance from the unseen world.

times, though, the sick people themselves have dreams and visions in which it is revealed to them, who or what made them sick.

Treatment of Sickness

The treatment of sickness has already been mentioned shortly in the previous section. People normally first use the public health care system, or, alternatively, use some traditional approaches that are not connected to the spirit world; i.e., herbal medicine, or specialists who deal with injuries of the bones, muscles or joints.

If this is of no avail, they call the family together, look for disunity and reconcile; believing that the reconciliation will help the sick person to get well again. If the ancestors are believed to have sent the sickness, they are asked to restore health. If a curse was spoken, it needs to be reversed.

If the sick person still does not recover, a traditional healer with access to the spirit world is called to help (usually after having consulted a diviner to find out from the spiritual realm who or what caused the sickness). The traditional healers often use lime, ginger, and/or body parts of the deceased through which the spirits are believed to exercise their power. In one ritual I witnessed, a woman who was sick "saw" in a dream that other women had used sorcery against her. She called the traditional healer who had lime in a plastic container. There was also a tooth of his deceased grandfather in the container. He marked various body parts of the sick woman with the lime, and then blew the powder towards her. The idea was that in the unseen world the spirit of his grandfather would fight the powers of sorcery and if he wins, the woman's health would be restored.

Sometimes, herbs, barks, roots and other materials from the bush are also used by traditional healers. Some of these materials may contain a medically effective substance, but they are also rather than not "loaded" with spiritual power. In many animistic contexts no clear distinction is being made between what is "spiritual" and what is purely "natural." At least for Manus, the means that are being used are better understood to lie on a continuum rather than that they could be placed into two separate categories.[7]

---

[7] In the next steps of my research, I will ask Christians on Manus how they evaluate the traditional concepts of sickness and healing from a Christian point of view. They might also be able to shed more light on these somehow ambiguous practices that employ the mentioned bush materials.

Considerations for Christian Health Ministry in Animistic Contexts

It is easy to imagine that when people from Western and from animistic contexts meet or work together, that they will interpret sickness in different ways and also take different approaches to find healing. In what follows, I offer five points to consider for people from a Western background who work among people in an animistic context; especially in the area of sickness and healing.[8]

1. Learning to understand people's beliefs and practices

When people want to work in a cultural setting different from their own, there is a need for them to study people's beliefs and practices phenomenologically.[9] This involves suspending one's judgement about what people say, do or believe. Only then will people open up and be willing to share how they understand their world, including their perceptions of sickness and healing.[10] Well-educated missionaries, health- or development workers from the West must take a conscious effort not to speak too much or even correct people's perspective at the beginning, lest they miss the chance to gain an understanding of life from the perspective of the people they want to serve.

Oftentimes, well-intended efforts to help people in their situation end up fruitless because the systems of understanding do not match. Understanding people's world is therefore a presupposition to help them adequately.

In addition, the professional from the West will often work with local or national co-workers, who bring their worldview or concepts with them.

---

[8] Beyond that, these points are equally relevant for those who work with people who come from such a context and are now living in the West (e.g., many of the refugees who have come to live in Europe in the recent years).

[9] This is the first step in Paul Hiebert's model of Critical Contextualization (1987), which provides very helpful advice for doing Christian ministry outside one's home culture.

[10] When I started research, I was concerned that people would not be willing to share their understanding and perspectives with me. I was encouraged by other researchers not to be shy, but to take people seriously in what they tell me. This proofed to be the key for me to gain understanding of the Lele's traditional health concept. If researchers (or health professionals, development workers, etc.) come with a desire to understand and not to judge, many people are willing to give them an insight into their world.

Not to understand their concepts will lead to ineffective collaboration and create tensions among the team (Käser, 1998).

2. Acknowledging that people see the world from different perspectives

It needs to be acknowledged that people in animistic contexts experience reality differently from how people in the West experience it. Their perspective needs to be taken seriously. Epistemologically it is a contested question whether it makes sense to speak of "their" reality as different from someone else's. But there is probably common ground in agreeing that people understand the world they live in from different angles (or with different spectacles on, to use another metaphor). People who want to reach out to others, need to start where these people are, not where they themselves are. People can connect something new only on the basis of what they already know (Shaw, 2010). In order for people to interpret or make sense of what they hear, they need to find the connectors to the world they know and they are living in.

At the same time people who come from the outside need to realize that they also have their "cultural prisons" they live in (Lingenfelter, 1986, 25). They, too, look at the world from a certain perspective. This does not mean that they have to accept other people's interpretation of the world and of what they experience as being ontologically true (Hiebert et al., 1999, 159). Nevertheless, it should make them sensitive and humble when dealing with people who have patterns of explanation and reasoning that are different from their own.

3. Dealing with sickness in a holistic way

For people in animistic contexts, sickness is more than a physical or mental dysfunction. It involves relationships, the unseen world, the questions of "sin," responsibilities, punishment, etc. The mention of "sin" is not so much to do with a deviation from the highest being's moral laws but the disturbance of peace and unity within the clan or the breaking of a taboo.

If people in animistic contexts get sick, they are often convinced that there is more involved than only a physical and/or a mental component. There are often also "religious" connotations (Käser, 1998, 240) in people's perception of sickness (e.g., seeing sickness as a sort of punishment for misbehavior or as an attack of the spirit world). For people who are Christians, sometimes the Christian god has taken the place of the moral instance of the ancestors and is seen as sending sickness.

At many places Western missionaries were at the forefront of bringing health-services to the people. But they have often de-coupled health ministry from religion and faith and have secularized it. It can be questioned how much of that was biblical and how much of it was the orientation of their own culture.[11] In the secularized thinking of the West there is no place for the middle zone with regard to sickness and healing and only a limited place for the role God is playing in it.

Especially for dealing with people in animistic contexts, there is a need to develop a holistic understanding and holistic practices concerning sickness and healing. From a biblical point of view, God (and Satan) are not only active in (what is sometimes called) the spiritual area (e.g., temptations, guidance, protecting from and leading into sin, etc.). God, as the creator, also sustains life. He cares for his people. He lets rain fall and crops grow. Can a good God also send sickness? Many people in Papua New Guinea would clearly answer in the affirmative. But they hold the same to be true for other powers and spirit-beings as well. People in animistic contexts see the different aspects of life as closely interconnected and the spiritual realm closely connected to the natural world. Those who come from the outside to serve these people do well to be mindful of their own dichotomies into which they have often divided their world.

From a Christian perspective, this also includes acknowledging that God works through the natural world. Therefore medicine does have its rightful place in dealing with sickness. What happens on Manus is that if people do not receive help through the public health system, they are very quick to attribute the sickness to the spirit world. Instead of taking a second look or trying another medicine, they quickly go and see the traditional healer. In that way they do not exhaust the range of medical treatment that could be tried out. It is also an easy escape door for medical professionals to tell people that they are not able to help, because the cause of the sickness has to lie in the traditional system.

Bryant Myers (2011, 101) has developed the following illustration:

---

[11] I cannot deal with the biblical concepts of sickness and healing in this article, but it is clear that in the Old Testament sickness often carried these religious connotations and in the New Testament these ideas are at least sporadically present (e.g., John 5:14; 1Cor. 11:30). For further study, see the classics as Seybold and Müller (1978) and Wilkinson (1998) and the newer studies by Scharfenberg (2005) and Gaiser (2010); here especially chapter 15 where he deals with the connection of sickness and sin on the example of Mark 2:1-12.

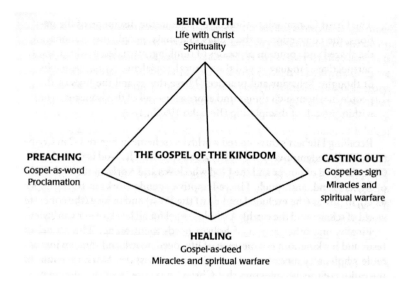

He notes that if Christians want to be witnesses of Christ's kingdom, they have to be with Jesus. This aspect is put at the top of the pyramid on purpose. Being with Jesus provides the Christian with his identity. But then, there are three other components and with any one of these missing, there is something missing in the understanding of the kingdom of God. Of course there is preaching as the proclamation of the good news and the salvation that is found in Jesus Christ. But there is also the dimension of the gospel as deed, which shows that God is concerned with the physical, social, and psychological well-being of people. And there is also the dimension of casting out demons and setting people free from their oppressions. This, he writes, is a sign of God's power and victory over darkness and all powers of evil.

From a Christian mission perspective, people in animistic societies, who are fearful of spirits and their power, need to see the signs of God's power. They need to experience that God is stronger than the sorcery that they believe has been used against them and stronger than the curses that might have been spelled out to harm them. The three dimensions on the bottom of the pyramid are not in itself the gospel of the kingdom without the top of the pyramid. On the other hand, a presentation of the gospel that lacks one of the lower dimensions is also less than complete.

At another place, Myers (2015) illustrates his point on the example of a hospital in Kenya that has as its motto: "We treat; Jesus heals." He makes it clear that the service of treating sick people is connected with the faith that it is God who cares about people and draws near to them.

With this being said, an issue that needs to be considered is how Christians can have a holistic health ministry without being manipulative. Whereas they will point out, if possible and appropriate, that it is God who heals and invite people to come into contact with him, they must never misuse the weakness of the sick in an attempt to convert them.

4. Opening doors for God's transformation

This point is the necessary attempt to balance what has been laid out in the previous point. Christians who work in animistic contexts need to help people to let God transform their understanding, their beliefs and practices. Although it is true that people can only build on what they already know and therefore need to connect new thoughts to their old ones, the Christian faith has always been a transforming factor in the lives of people. This entails to encourage people to discover reality from God's perspective which can lead to a critique of their own beliefs and practices in light of God's word and in community. One example is to discover God as the creator and sustainer of life so that trust in God dominates over fear of sorcery. Christians who work among people with animistic orientation will do well to ask themselves whether their own responses to people's beliefs and practices affirm systems that are destructive for life (e.g., in upholding the fear of sorcery) or if there are other ways that not only lead to new behavior in a given situation but leads to a transformation of people's underlying beliefs and understandings.[12] The Willowbank Report rightly points out: "As we address Scripture, Scripture addresses us. We find that our culturally conditioned presuppositions are being challenged and our questions corrected. In fact, we are compelled to reformulate our previous questions and to ask fresh ones" (Lausanne Committee for World Evangelization, 1978, 11).

People who profess to be Christians should be led to a point where they ask the question: "What does it mean that we are God's people and that God is dwelling in our midst?" God, as revealed in scripture, has always had the desire to be with people, in their daily lives. When people begin to understand themselves as the people of God and grasp that God is present with them in their situation (including the times of droughts, sickness, or death), then the way to a transformation on a deeper level of their lives begins to open up (Shaw & van Engen, 2003).

A practical way to lead people into transformation is to develop meaningful rituals. People in animistic societies often live their lives not individually but collectively. In addition, transformation does not always start on a

---

[12] For further reflection on this points, see Shorter (1985, 93–104).

cognitive level. Therefore, to develop Christ-honoring, communal practices (incl. rituals) to deal with sickness, is an essential step towards transformation. In their traditional practices, coming together and performing a ritual for healing (as for many other areas of life), was common practice. Christians from the West, especially Protestants, often have very little sense for rituals. People are told to pray in times of need, but they often long for signs that undergird beliefs and express their faith in more tangible ways. In the Bible, the advice found in James 5:14-16 to pray over a sick person together and anoint the person with oil, serves as an example of taking care of the sick in a communal way that adds a sign to the words spoken in prayer.

5. Strengthening communities to face hardship together

In order to tackle the hard times of life together, people need functioning communities. Shortly before I left Manus, a couple of people told me, independently of each other, that the wife of one pastor went to see a traditional healer to get rid of a demon she believed troubled her. She had back pain for a long time and could not find any other help. Instead of providing an opportunity for the woman to talk about her pain, her anxieties and her fears, people started to talk *about* her. Congregations, women and youth groups have the potential to become places where people find support in times of crises. This potential is being utilized if people can talk freely about their problems and struggles, including their sicknesses, and find the support of a strong, caring community that stands together when individuals suffer.

One of the most encouraging things we have done in the church on Manus was to let people testify how God has helped them in times of sickness and demonic oppressions. Once, after I had preached about the man possessed by evil spirits (Luke 8:26-39), one of the Bible school students shared her testimony. She told that oftentimes when she lay down to sleep, she felt an evil power "sitting" on her chest and making it hard for her to breath, let alone sleep. Whenever this happened she went to one of the Bible school teachers to pray for her and over time it got better. People in animistic contexts need examples where the power of God is at work in the life of people as an encouragement to trust God in their sickness and oppression as well. We have made good experiences with inviting older people to share how they lived their lives as children of God and how they experienced God's help in times of sickness. One older man told the congregation how people related his sickness to the attack of a sorcerer and encouraged him to use counter-sorcery, which he refused, because he wanted to trust Christ's power alone. These times of giving testimony became an encouragement for many of the younger people in the church.

Working for strong and supporting communities also entails to help people to renew their trust to each other by confessing jealousy, hatred, envy, fear, and receiving forgiveness. Ill feelings against each other are the nursing ground for evil actions and witchcraft accusations. But when these are removed, people can start to trust, support, and love each other and live together as a caring Christian community that exercises a positive influence on the community as a whole (Hiebert et al., 1999).

Conclusion

Christians who cross cultural boundaries and are confronted with animistic beliefs and practices among the people they want to serve will often be challenged in their own assumptions. Hiebert, Shaw and Tiénou point out that the Gospel challenges a modern secular worldview just as it challenges a magical, animistic worldview. "The Bible ... calls people to entrust themselves to the care of the God of righteousness and love. The gospel offers them much more than health and success on earth. It gives them shalom in the fullest sense of the word" (1999, 159). This is what is to be gained for people from all kinds of different cultural contexts, who start to put their trust in God—in the good times of life as well as in times of hardship and sickness.

Bibliography

Gaiser, F. J. (2010). *Healing in the Bible. Theological insight for Christian ministry*. Grand Rapids, MI: Baker Academic.

Harvey, G. (2006). *Animism. Respecting the living world*. New York, NY: Columbia University Press.

Hiebert, P. G. (1982). The flaw of the excluded middle. *Missiology, 10(1)*, 35–47.

_____. (1987). Critical contextualization. *International Bulletin of Missionary Research, 11(3)*, 104–112.

Hiebert, P. G., Shaw, R. D., & Tiénou, T. (1999). *Understanding folk religion. A Christian response to popular beliefs and practices*. Grand Rapids, MI: Baker.

Käser, L. (1998). *Fremde Kulturen. Eine Einführung in die Ethnologie für Entwicklungshelfer und kirchliche Mitarbeiter in Übersee*. Bad Liebenzell: Verlag der Liebenzeller Mission.

―――――. (2004). *Animismus. Eine Einführung in die begrifflichen Grundlagen des Welt- und Menschenbildes traditionaler (ethnischer) Gesellschaften für Entwicklungshelfer und kirchliche Mitarbeiter in Übersee*. Bad Liebenzell: Verlag der Liebenzeller Mission.

―――――. (2014). *Animism. A Cognitive Approach. An Introduction to the Basic Notions* (D. Cheeseman, Trans.). Nürnberg: VTR.

Lausanne Committee for World Evangelization. (1978). *The Willowbank Report: Consultation on Gospel and Culture*, Wheaton, IL; available at: https://www.lausanne.org/content/lop/lop-2.

Lingenfelter, S. G., and Marvin K. Mayers (1986). *Ministering cross-culturally. An incarnational model for personal relationships*. Grand Rapids, MI: Baker Academic.

Morgan, G. R. (2012). *Understanding World Religions in 15 Minutes a Day*. Minneapolis, MN: Bethany House Publishers.

Myers, B. L. (2011). *Walking with the poor. Principles and practices of transformational development. Revised and Updated ed.* Maryknoll, NY: Orbis.

Myers, B. L. (2015). Announcing the whole gospel: Health, healing and Christian witness. In B. L. Myers, E. E. Dufault-Hunter, & I. Voss (Eds.), *Health, healing, and shalom. Frontiers and challenges for Christian health missions*. Pasadena: William Carey Library.

Scharfenberg, R. (2005). *Wenn Gott nicht heilt. Theologische Schlaglichter auf ein seelsorgerliches Problem*. Nürnberg: VTR.

Seybold, K., & Müller, U. B. (1978). *Krankheit und Heilung* (Vol. 1008). Stuttgart: Kohlhammer.

Shaw, R. D. (2010). Beyond contextualization. Toward a twenty-first century model for enabling mission. *International Bulletin of Missionary Research, 34(4)*, 208–212.

Shaw, R. D., & van Engen, C. E. (2003). *Communicating God's Word in a complex world. God's truth or hocus pocus?* Lanham, MD: Rowman & Littlefield Publishers.

Shorter, A. (1985). *Jesus and the witchdoctor. An approach to healing and wholeness*. Maryknoll, NY: Orbis Books.

Wilkinson, J. (1998). *The Bible and healing. A medical and theological commentary*. Grand Rapids, MI: William B. Eerdmans.

Contributors

Saúl Cruz-Valdivieso, M.A. Clinical Psychology; Assistant Director of Organización Armonía, A.C., Mexico.

Kathryn A. Cummins, B.A., Program Coordinator of the Institute for International Care and Counsel, Belhaven University, Jackson, Mississippi, USA.

Ulrich Giesekus, Prof. Dr., Prof. of Psychology and Counseling, Liebenzell Internationale Hochschule (University of Applied Sciences).

Simon Herrmann, B.A., Missionary on Manus Island, Papua New Guinea, doctoral student (Ph.D. Intercultural Studies) at Fuller Theological Seminary, Pasadena (CA).

Beate Jakob, M.D., Consultant for Theological Studies on Health and Healing, German Institute for Medical Mission (DIFAEM, Tübingen, Germany).

Gladys K. Mwiti, Ph.D. in Clinical Psychology, Founder & CEO Oasis Africa Center for Transformational Psychology & Trauma, Kenya.

Samuel Pfeifer, Prof. Dr. med., Riehen/Marburg.

Bradford M. Smith, Ph.D., Director of the Institute for International Care and Counsel, Belhaven University, Jackson, Mississippi, USA.